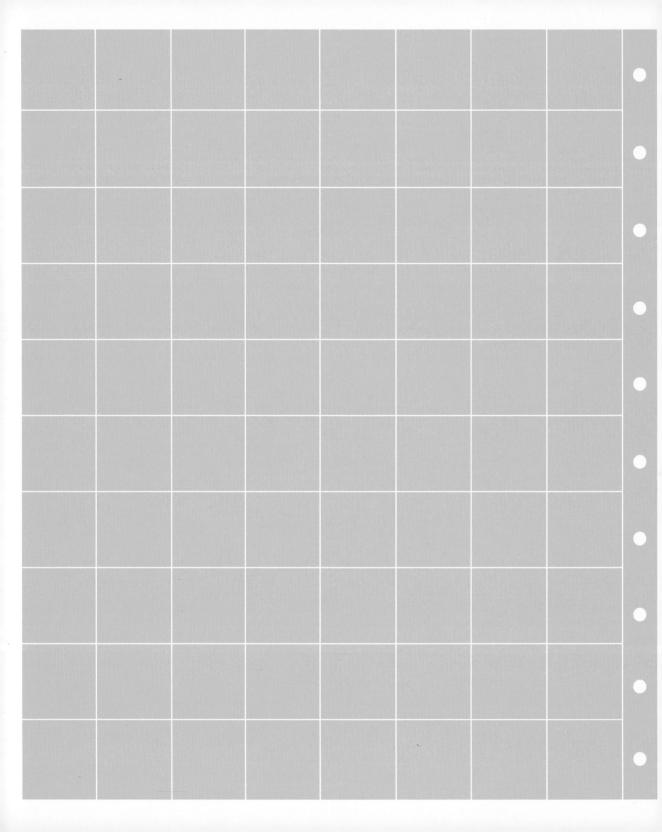

Sustainable
adjective Pertaining to a system that maintains its own viability by using techniques that allow for continual reuse.

Gifting
noun Something given voluntarily without payment in return, as to show favour toward someone, honour an occasion, or make a gesture of assistance.

Upcycle, hand-make & get creative with
zero-waste presents & packages

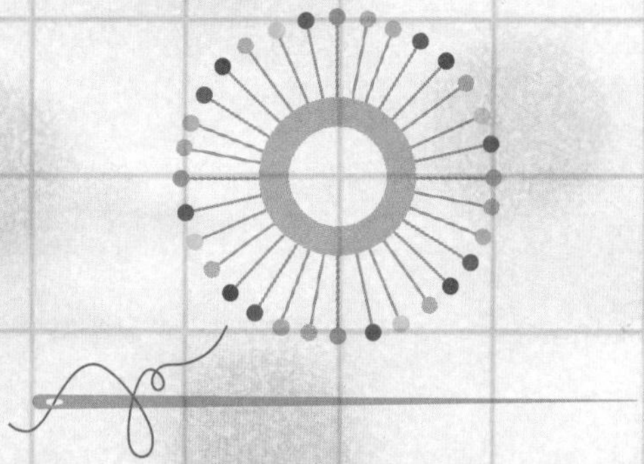

SUSTAINABLE GIFTING

MICHELLE
MACKINTOSH

Hardie Grant

BOOKS

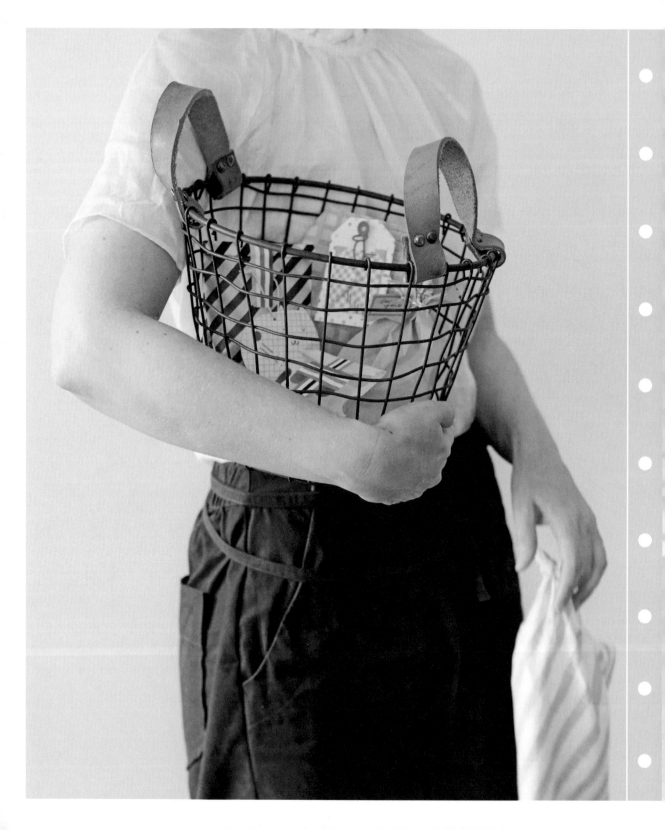

Contents

Introduction

GREEN GIFTING

on making
a difference

In today's busy world, it can be hard to find the time to stop, plan and make rather than rush out and buy. There are many opportunities to gift loved ones: not just birthdays and Christmas and times of celebration but also when things are tough. Sustainable gifting is a choice to leave a smaller carbon footprint. To make rather than buy, or buy with the planet in mind.

This book is for all the citizen makers who want to live in a kinder world, without the latest gadget or must-have item. This book is for people who want to slow down, think about who they are gifting to and make a present from the heart. A gift with minimal impact on the planet, that is all about thought, not all about money.

The gifts you make will be no less significant – on the contrary, they will be received with surprise and delight. You took time. You made something from the heart. You thought about your friend but also the planet. This is the way the new, kinder world works. It's part old-school but also completely new..

Welcome to the world of sustainable gifting. Once you enter, there is no turning back. It's a new way of looking at the world. Respect for nature, family, local and global communities. Each action we take can make a difference.

If we all take these small steps our impact will be enormous. So please join me on this quest.

In a world where the climate emergency is top of mind, everyday decisions need to be made with a thought to sustainability and a move away from single use items.

Gifting something handmade provides a unique opportunity to spend time and thought creating for a loved one using upcycled, natural or raw materials that fit your code of ethics.

When thinking of something to craft, bake or make and buying from a store, consider if it is made locally – try to buy from small-batch makers – or buy from a local store not a chain. And don't forget to use what you have yourself, like eggs from your own hens, or plants, flowers and seeds from your garden.

I designed this furoshiki with uguisustore.com in Tokyo

What makes a great sustainable gift?

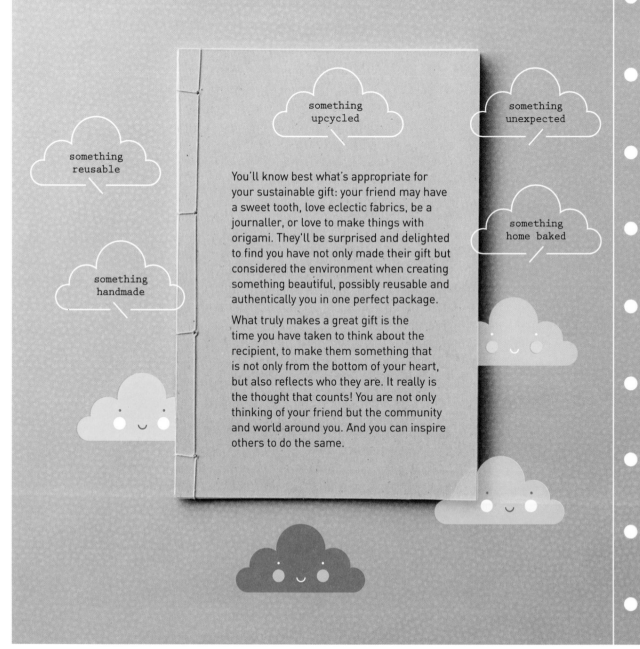

something upcycled

something unexpected

something reusable

something home baked

something handmade

You'll know best what's appropriate for your sustainable gift: your friend may have a sweet tooth, love eclectic fabrics, be a journaller, or love to make things with origami. They'll be surprised and delighted to find you have not only made their gift but considered the environment when creating something beautiful, possibly reusable and authentically you in one perfect package.

What truly makes a great gift is the time you have taken to think about the recipient, to make them something that is not only from the bottom of your heart, but also reflects who they are. It really is the thought that counts! You are not only thinking of your friend but the community and world around you. And you can inspire others to do the same.

Before you buy a box, tin, jar or vintage suitcase, or think about making your package out of paper or fabric, you'll need to decide on the delivery method that suits your project and recipient best, as this will affect how large your parcel is and what you include in it.

When planning a gift I firstly think about what my friend may want or need, what I could make them, or give them that they could reuse, have for a short time (homemade baking) or a long time (a plant for their garden).

I think about how I am going to package it, for example could part of the present be the wrapping – a teatowel to wrap a cake for example (see page 62).

If I need supplies I try to buy locally and thoughtfully to support local makers or innovators if I can.

I keep pretty wrapping paper to reuse, or any kind of interesting packing paper. I dry flowers and leaves and collect lots of twine and stickers. So I'll always be able to pretty up anything I make in a hurry.

THE FOLLOWING ARE THINGS TO CONSIDER WHEN PLANNING A GIFT

Would they appreciate baking?

Will the receiver use the item/s?

Can part of the present be the clever way it is wrapped, or can part of the gift be used for another purpose?

If I know a birthday or occasion is coming up I'll buy supplies from an ethical supplier to make something, or plan a trip to a farmer's market or craft store to gather all the components of my gift-making project.

As the saying goes, it's what's on the inside that counts. You don't need to spend a lot of money on lavish gifts to make somebody feel loved and cared for. An afternoon's worth of baking, a piece of paper ingeniously folded, music lovingly curated: all these won't break the bank, and yet they are such simple and sustainable presents. (Of course, sometimes, for the right person on the right occasion, you do just need to go all out!) In this chapter, you'll find some of my favourite items to gift to others. Pick and mix whatever takes your fancy, find inspiration and put your own personal spin on things for all of the people you cherish.

No time like
the present

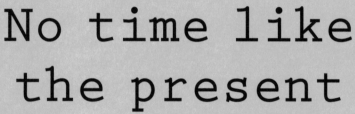

Crafting a present

Making something beautiful, ethical and sustainable is a chance to get super-creative: the most interesting gifts contain surprises and memories, and can tell stories without words. Choose a theme and see where it takes you — anything goes, so long as you consider the recipient's favourite colours, scents, foods, hobbies, and taste and style. A present can contain multiple items.

Instead of using a standard cardboard box to house your gifts, why not upcycle something that suits your loved one's personality, aesthetic or sense of humour? Milk crates, drawstring bags, wooden wine crates and produce tins all make great gift boxes. Perhaps he or she is not into material things? Bake some bread and wrap it up with homemade jam and freshly ground coffee or a favourite tea – a romantic breakfast for two!

If your object of affection is a little out of the box, get creative when it comes to presentation. You could turn your present into a cryptic puzzle, with individually wrapped items. Tag one item with the number one and a clue to which parcel to open next. If your love adores mysteries, why not turn the whole thing into a treasure hunt for the location of the parcel? Each step of the journey could be rewarded with a small token or souvenir of your relationship (or chocolate!).

If it's a big statement you want to make, have the package delivered to their workplace or school for a seriously romantic public declaration (but make sure the recipient is not too shy and retiring to appreciate it).

Think of this as an opportunity to show just how much you know and care: whether the parcel is simple or elaborate, big or small, it should speak to who the recipient is, inside and out.

Ideas for gifts

a handmade card
(see page 36)
or letter

origami hearts
(see page 25)

a USB stick
containing a mix of
music memories

a photo book
(see page 50)

a favourite vintage
childhood toy you've
tracked down online

a favourite old
book with a new
personalised cover

safety
pins

buttons
and
stickers

clips

confetti

wooden
buttons and
beads

pressed
flowers

coasters

peg
hooks

feathers
and pom poms

wooden
pegs

rosebud
tea and
dried
flora

gold
and
silver
clips

craft shop
letters

beautifully
designed
stamps

muslin
bags

fabric
buttons

tags

paper
doilies

paper
clips

linen
thread

daruma
thread

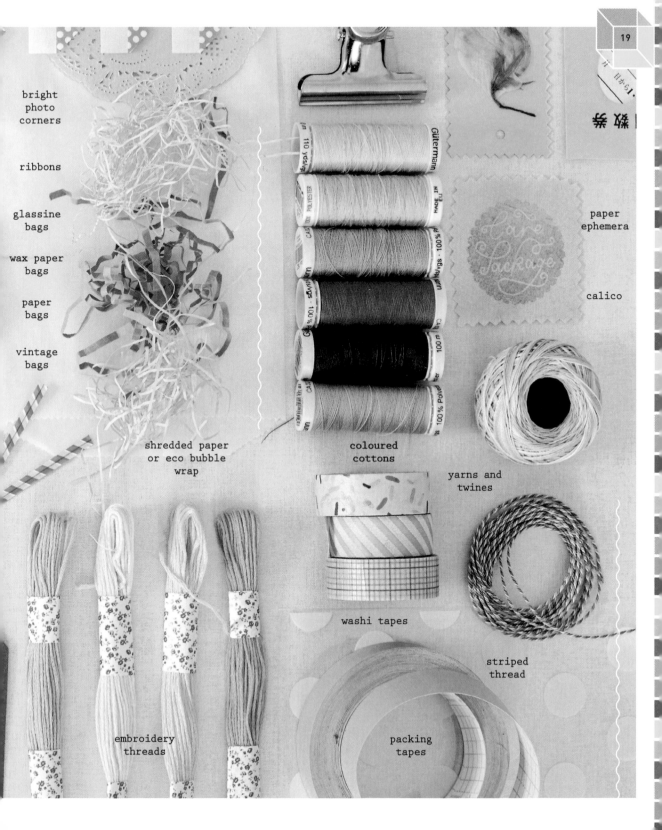

bright
photo
corners

ribbons

glassine
bags

wax paper
bags

paper
bags

vintage
bags

shredded paper
or eco bubble
wrap

coloured
cottons

paper
ephemera

calico

yarns and
twines

washi tapes

striped
thread

embroidery
threads

packing
tapes

Bon bons

I've filled my bonbon with sweets and wrapped it with wax paper, washi tape and personalised stickers

you could include chocolate truffles (see page 72)

You ALWAYS make me smile

I hope you know how much you mean to me

| toilet paper tubes (or garbage bag tubes) | wax paper or recycled wrapping paper | washi tape stickers bonbon fillings |

This is a fun project to make with little ones for any celebration. It's super easy and a great creative way of using things around the house. I use square sandwich wax paper as you just need to give the ends a little twist and they stay fixed. Paper also works well; however, you'll need to tie each end with some twine.

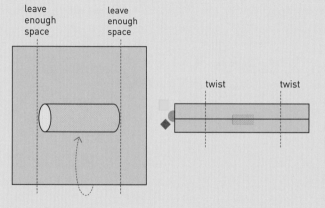

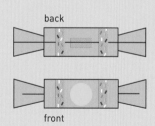

leave enough space   leave enough space

twist   twist

back

front

Lay your tube in the middle of a square piece of wax or recycled paper. Make sure you have enough room at each end to twist the bonbon.

Roll the wax paper tightly around the tube and seal nicely with washi tape. Making sure the tube is centred, twist one end of the wax paper just once. Add your bonbon filling (a small letter, sweets or toys), then twist the second end neatly just once.

I always wrap washi tape around the whole bonbon, near each end, then place a circular sticker in the centre. I add the person's name to the sticker or a personal note or quote.

Washi tape alphabet

rule up your own
graph paper the
same width as the
washi tape

A a b C c
D d E F G
H I J K L
M N O o

P q Q R r
S T F U u
V v W X
Y y Z z

I've used a mix
of navy, yellow
and green

use the alphabet
to create labels
and names

If you're like me and have what most would call an unhealthy obsession with washi tape (Japanese paper tape), this project is a perfect way to justify your purchases.

Simply choose a colour combination for decorating your parcel, grab some graph paper and arrange strips of washi tape to make names or phrases. I used a skinny washi tape that matched the width of the graph paper and use embroidery scissors for precision. It takes a bit of practice, but definitely pays off!

make cute graphpaper notebooks

I used MT branded tapes

perfect for birthday or anniversary tags

Origami mobiles

type a letter
and fold it into an
origami heart

cut
washi tape
into flags

mix
vintage papers
with brights

pop
tiny notes
under each flap at
the back of your hearts

| origami paper or squares of recycled or vintage paper | washi tape

natural twine | a clothes hanger (wooden, vintage or a cute shape) |

Origami mobiles are a wonderful way to brighten up a room. While these would be perfect for a mother and baby, I think they are a lovely gift for all ages. You can also use the hearts and stars to decorate gifts.

1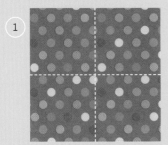

Fold the square into quarters and unfold.

2

Turn over. Fold the bottom edge up to the middle fold.

3

Turn over again. Fold the bottom corners so they meet in the centre.

4

Turn over again. Fold the sides so they meet in the centre.

5

Fold in the top left and right corners to form a peak. Without folding, carefully bring the top point down to meet the bottom point.

6

Carefully flatten to create two inward-pointing triangles at the top of the shape. Fold down the top right and top left corners.

7

Tuck the front point of the heart into the pocket behind it.

8

Fold down the top points and flip over to complete the heart shape!

Tape twine to the back of the hearts and affix to the hanger with washi tape.

1

With the wrong side facing up, fold each piece of paper diagonally and open back up.

2

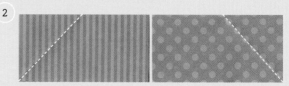

Fold in half as shown, so the right side of the paper is now facing up. Open the paper back up.

3

4

Turn the paper 180° and fold in half as shown.

5

Following the existing diagonal crease in the paper, fold the bottom edge up so it meets the centre crease. Fold the top edge down to meet the centre crease.

6

Flip the pieces over. Fold the top and bottom peaks as shown.

7

Fold down the bottoms and tops to make the shapes shown. Allow the bottoms and tops to unfold.

8

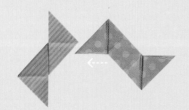

Flip the right shape over and position the two pieces as shown. Lay the left piece on top of the right piece so the vertical edges run parallel to the right shape's folds.

9

Fold the top shape at the dotted lines and tuck the points into the pockets at the back of the bottom shape.

10

Fold and tuck the points of the bottom shape into the pockets of the top shape. Voilà!

Rubber stamps

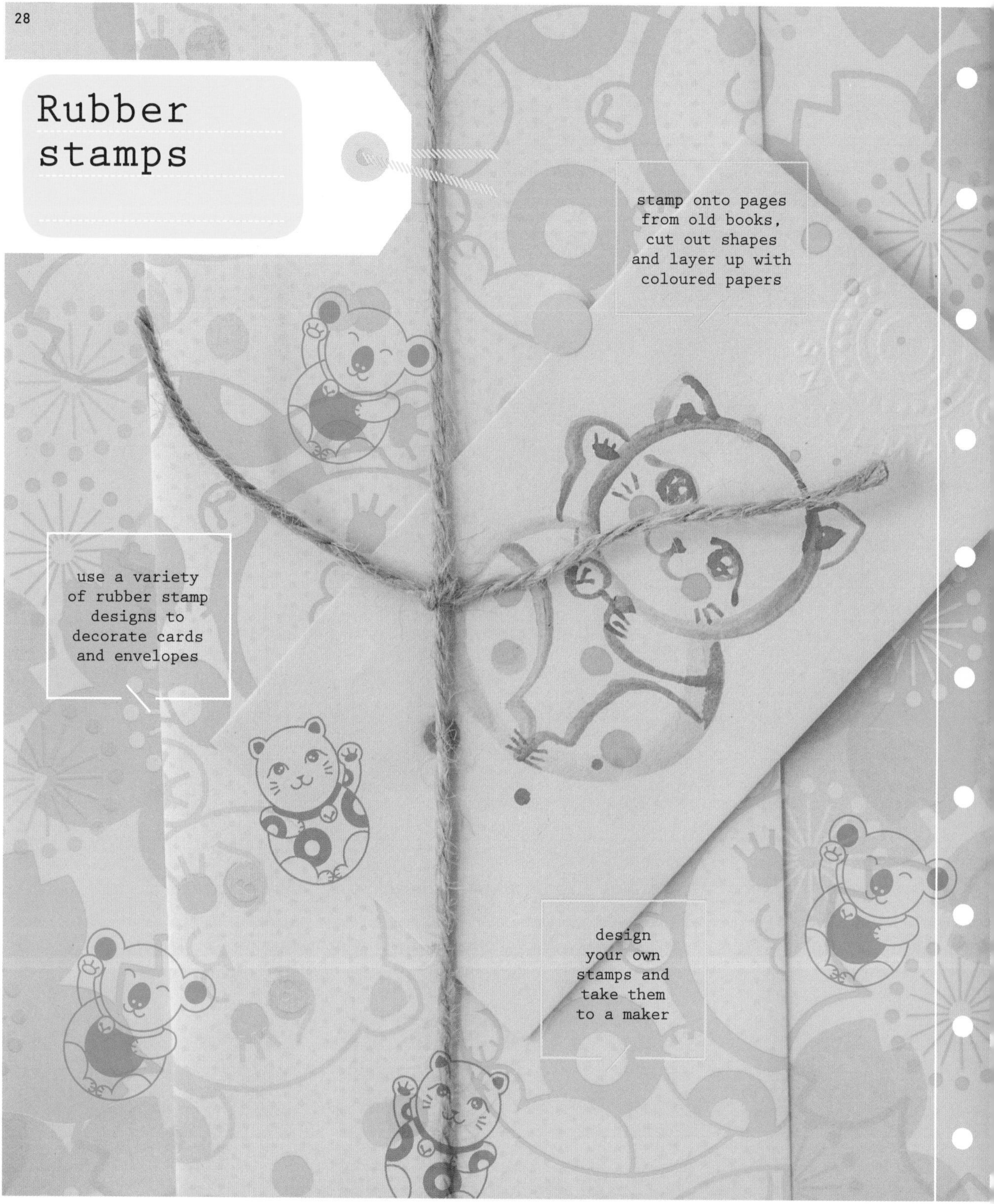

stamp onto pages
from old books,
cut out shapes
and layer up with
coloured papers

use a variety
of rubber stamp
designs to
decorate cards
and envelopes

design
your own
stamps and
take them
to a maker

I'm a huge fan of rubber stamps. You can use them over and over again and experiment by stamping onto different sorts of fabrics, papers and recycled materials. I love making labels and tags by stamping onto calico and hand stitching edges.

You can find some stamps I've designed for you to take to a professional stamp-maker on page 31 (it's a relatively inexpensive exercise), as well as some designs that you can carve yourself, using an eraser or a rubber sheet from your local art supplier. It takes a little bit of confidence and practice but once you get going it's highly addictive and oh-so-therapeutic. My stamp-maker makes wooden stamps of the most beautiful quality out of my designs. I must confess to dreaming up new designs all the time and then somehow justifying having them made.

Visit your local art or craft shop for some interesting ink colours and investigate fabric inks if you are thinking of stamping onto fabric.

Decorated calico bags

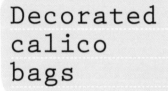

why not stitch a simple fabric design onto calico?

make a woodland design on your bag using different coloured inks

To carve your own stamps, buy a carving or linocut tool set suitable for rubber, as well as some rubber blocks (or else you can carve your design into erasers). Trace or draw your design onto the rubber and, with your tool nearly parallel to the surface, start carving. Use a larger tool to carve away the edges. Be careful as carving tools are very sharp!

manekineko stamp
is made from the cover
of a book I co-wrote
called *Tokyo Pocket
Precincts*

manekikoala stamp
was made for an
exhibition in Tokyo
at Galerie Doux
Dimanche

HOME
MADE

Bound paper journals

try making versions with more or fewer holes

use a round tag or coaster and pierce to make a threaded tag

There are so many ways to make a journal. Try this beautifully simple hand-binding technique for a thoroughly elegant approach. If you want to use thicker twine you'll need bigger holes in your paper.

this Japanese twine changes colour from teal to pink

1 piece of thick A4 card for front and back of journal scalpel, bone folder and cutting mat

15 pieces of A4 paper for internals, including recycled materials needle and thread or twine

book binding awl (paper stabber) bulldog clip, pencil and ruler

1

Take the piece of A4 card and cut it in half to make 2 × A5 pieces of card. Using a bone folder or the back of your scalpel to make sharp folds, fold the A4 paper pieces in half.

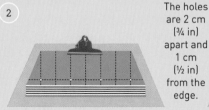

2

Sandwich the internal pages between the pieces of card, aligning the edges. Clamp together with a bulldog clip, placing it on the edge side of the journal, not the spine (fold) side. Mark in pencil the four places you will pierce holes.

The holes are 2 cm (¾ in) apart and 1 cm (½ in) from the edge.

3

Working on a cutting mat, use the book binding awl to pierce the four marked places all the way through the front cover, pages and back cover. Make sure the holes are big enough for your needle to go through.

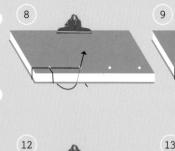

4

Following the diagrams, sew the pages together with the needle and thread.

5

6

7

8

9

10

11

12

13

14

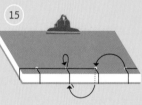

15

Sew back into the last hole and tie a knot at the back to secure.

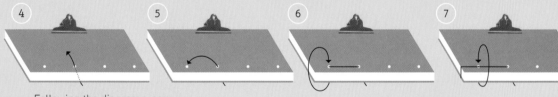

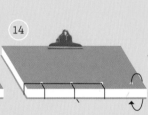

fold a pocket
A6 journal
cover

receipt

received
from

Michelle
Mackintosh

for a pretty
cover, paint dots
onto watercolour
paper

use
ring binders
to hold your
journal
together

add envelopes
and tabs

make a tag and
hang it from
your journal

stitch down
the middle
of your paper
and cover

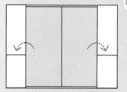

1

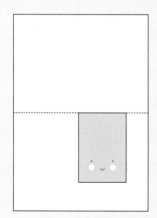

You'll need a piece of A3 paper and an A6 journal (or 10 × A5 pages stitched down the middle with a sewing machine). Fold the A3 sheet in half to make a rectangle the size of an A4 sheet of paper.

2

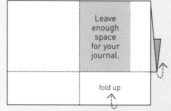

Leave enough space for your journal.

fold up

Fold in half again to make a rectangle the size of an A5 sheet, then unfold. Align the journal as shown, then fold the excess paper at the bottom of the sheet up to make pockets.

3

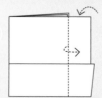

Fold the excess paper around the front and back of the journal to create flaps.

4

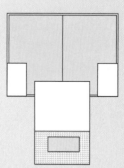

Tuck the front and back of the journal into the pocket flaps to secure the cover.

5

Decorate the pocket!

Cards
and paper
additions

create a
paper-cut
collage on the
front of a
journal

pop the
journal in
a muslin bag
with cute
tags

add a
matching ruler
and pen to the
package

do a collage on some recycled paper for a quick card design

fold hearts in half and glue half onto the card

try a simple watercolour design on cotton or art paper

try a repeat pattern and change up the faces

CONGRATS

make a mini flag with many colours

cat designs are always appropriate!

Fabric
journals

plain paper journal

fabric and calico to wrap your journal with

enough iron-on adhesive to fuse your fabric pieces

an iron

needle and thread

buttons, ribbons or twine, to embellish

This is a really stylish way to pretty up a plain paper journal. I love to use linen or heavy cotton fabrics, stitching the edges and decorating with buttons, ribbon, twine or string. These journals don't need to be feminine; a strong, graphic print or a simple colour combination works really well for a unisex or a more masculine design.

Open your journal up and place it on top of the fabric and calico. Trace a shape roughly 1 cm (½ in) larger than the journal, with 3 cm (1¼ in) extra on the left and right sides to form flaps.

Sandwich the iron-on adhesive between the two fabrics, pin and trim to the same size. Follow the instructions of the iron-on adhesive to fuse the fabrics together.

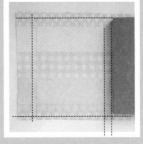

Measure and mark out the width and height of the spine, front and back of the journal, as well as the flaps. Align each part of the journal on the fabric to ensure it all fits. (This is crucial!)

Trim to size, making sure you leave 1 cm (½ in) at the top and bottom of the journal cover to prevent frayed edges. Iron down the flaps and the excess at the top and bottom.

Wrap around the journal, making sure everything fits snugly.

Hem the top and bottom edges of the journal cover with a needle and thread. Stitch a button to the front of the journal and wrap twine or ribbon around it to secure and finish.

make a furoshiki
bag out of a
handkerchief
or scarf (see
page 152)

hand-stitched
journal
(see page 39)

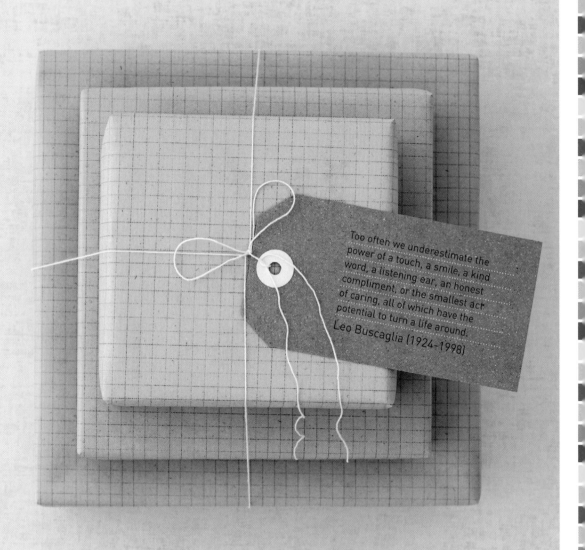

Too often we underestimate the power of a touch, a smile, a kind word, a listening ear, an honest compliment, or the smallest act of caring, all of which have the potential to turn a life around.

Leo Buscaglia (1924–1998)

Upcycled denim lunch bag

Melt equal parts jojoba oil and beeswax and combine in a jar. With a paintbrush paint the wax onto the inside of your bag. With a hairdryer on high, dry the wax; when dry, repeat with the front of the bag. Your bag is now waterproof! It will be stiff enough to sit up straight and hold food!

If you don't want to wax your bag, cut denim squares with pinking sheers and wax them, then wrap up a sandwich for your bag!

| a pair of jeans or pants you no longer need a cute button | a hair elastic (I like coloured ones but you could also use twine) | needle and thread pinking shears optional: sewing machine |

An old pair of pants lying around can be upcycled into a brilliant lunch box bag, storage bag or all-purpose handy bag around the house. It's an easy crafternoon project achieved with or without a sewing machine. You can fasten these bags in one of two ways: option one is shown below, option two, you cut the denim a little higher and roll down the fabric and fasten. You can make two or more bags per pair!

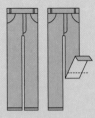

Inside out

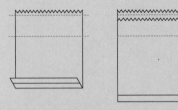

Lay your jeans out and fold one leg up and then fold the end of the jeans over 4 cm/ 1½ in (but any size will work). This will be the top of your bag. Pin in place.

Measure down 20 cm (8 in). Add an additional 9 cm (3½ in) for the base of your bag. Cut with pinking sheers.

Turn the piece inside out. Draw a line 5 mm (¼ in) from the end of the bag with a ruler and stitch (backstitch, see page 150, or use a sewing machine). Iron the edges flat.

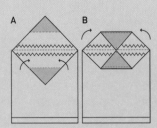

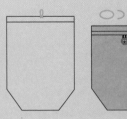

Fold the stitched edge into a diamond (see A). Make sure you have a neat shape as this is the base of your bag. Fold over again tucking triangles inward (see B). Stitch along the blue lines shown and turn the bag the right way around and tuck the base into place.

Cut your hair elastic in half, pinch into a loop and pin into the centre of the top of the top flap, fold and sew into the jean cuff's first layer (so you cannot see stitching on the outside of your bag). Fold and sew a button on the front of the bag to loop with the elastic.

Sashiko stitching

| embroidery thread and needle | vintage fabric scraps in linen and cotton | scissors |

This simple Japanese stitching technique comes from the highly creative Edo period (1603-1868). It looks wonderful on vintage indigo or neutral fabrics. There are quite a few stitches in this style; below are some of my favourites. When you get the hang of your favourite stitch, try adding some to the upcycled denim lunch bag (page 43). You can buy special sashiko needles and thread; however, any needles and pretty threads you have at home will do nicely. You can draw a pattern onto the interface and fuse it onto the back of your fabric for a perfect guide (there are lots of designs online); my preference is to keep it quite loose and creative, perfectly imperfect.

 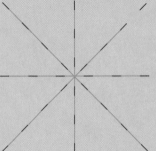 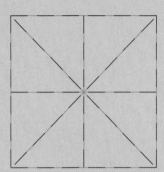

Stitching in a line, as above, is the best way to start. You can be a little wonky here, it just gives the design charm. Boro (making clothes from rags) uses a lot of this stitching in a really naive way, and can be a great source of inspiration for your first project.

The one serious rule for sashiko stitching is that all stitches should be the same size. The stitches on the back of your fabric should be half as long as the stitches on the front of your fabric; however, I personally like my smaller stitches on the front.

If you like a perfect stitch, this design en masse looks beautiful if you are stitching white onto indigo.

sashiko stitching looks great on visible mending patches

for more stitching ideas see page 150

A cute fabric bag should be in your everyday bag, or backpack, for an unexpected farmer's market or general shopping.

Fabrics like calico, cotton, linen or hemp, or any kind of raw materials, are the best kinds to use. Make your own or buy a plain one and craft it up.

Importantly we all need to stay away from single use plastic items and this is the best small step any of us can take to reduce global waste.

this makes a
sustainable
shopping bag

hand stitch tree
and house shapes
onto a calico bag

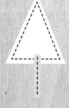

Gift a housewarming present in a 'house' bag. Food is packaged in reusable containers.

Paint the wine bottle in a matt pastel colour and reuse as a vase!

A little bit of hand stitching goes a long way!

Not only is it therapeutic but it makes each gift utterly unique.

You don't have to stitch up a storm like a Jane Austin character, just learn the basics and start with something small.

See page 150 for some of my favourite stitches.

NIVEA
Creme

handmade
Christmas
decorations

use iron-on
adhesive on your
fabric squares
for sturdiness

cut out fabric
squares and
hand stitch onto
a calico bag

Photo book ideas

use vintage paper corners to fix photos to thick cotton paper

Tokyo 2021

personalise with a rubber stamp letter set

try using an old analogue camera and processing

affix
a tiny envelope
and letter to
the front

biodegradable
party bag

start a love affair
with vintage cameras

wrap photos in
patterned greaseproof
paper and bind with
twine, beads and
washi tape

cut
natural board
into tag shapes
and ring-bind

use a
permanent
marker to
draw a vintage
camera onto a
muslin bag

use bright and
fun photo corners

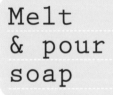

Melt
& pour
soap

make labels
listing the
scent, texture
and therapeutic
benefits

try setting
your soap in
different
shapes

package
soap in wax
paper and string,
rubber-stamped
brown paper and
ribbon, or tiny
boxes

vintage
sewing
patterns
pad out
the box

cut the
soaps with rough
edges for a
super-handmade
feel

use anything
for the moulds
from a cut-down
milk carton to
an ice-cream
container

450 g (1 lb) melt & pour soap base (available online or at health food stores)

soap moulds or a cake tin lined with baking paper

½ tablespoon of essential oil of your choice
seeds, flowers, etc

Making soap the traditional way is a bit of a tricky business due to the use of caustic soda. However, making soap from a melt-and-pour base, soap flakes or small pieces of leftover soap can be a wonderful afternoon project — and, when finished, will still look incredibly impressive. If you have a lovely garden or a cupboard full of oils, salts, seeds and spices, you may already have half the ingredients you need. This is a great project that allows you to get creative with colour, texture and scent. And packaging the soaps adds another dimension full of creative possibilities.

Cut your soap base into 1.5 cm (½ in) cubes and place in a large, oven-safe glass bowl. Microwave the soap base for 30 seconds, then for intervals of 15 seconds, stirring between bursts and checking to see when it is melted. Soap can burn, so keep an eye on it.

I like to make each soap a little different, so when the soap base is melted, I stir through the essential oil and divide it between several smaller bowls, then add any extra additions (for instance, coffee or poppy seeds). Pour the soap into the mould and decorate the tops if desired (I pop a whole coffee bean on my coffee-scented soap). If making several varieties of soap, try layering one on top of another for a lovely layered effect. Use a rounded knife or spatula to get rid of any small bubbles on top before the soap starts to set.

Remove the soap from the moulds after a couple of hours. Place onto a cake rack and leave overnight. Wrap beautifully for a present or store in an airtight container until you assemble your package.

TIP You can try this with soap flakes or grated left-over soap, but you may need to add a little cow, almond or soy milk to soften and help the flakes combine. Add 185 ml (6 fl oz/¾ cup) of milk to 450 g (1 lb) of soap and leave overnight before melting.

Tip When storing soap in an airtight container, use a layer of baking paper to separate each piece.

Tip A variety of soap bases are available. I like to use ones made from glycerine, shea butter and olive oil.

Optional extras
for exfoliation: salt, coffee, sugar, poppy seeds, almond meal

for deodorisation: coffee

for visual effect: dried lavender, mint, rosemary, thyme, poppy seeds

for moisturisation (start with a tablespoon; too much will prevent your soap from setting): aloe vera, shea butter, coconut oil, beeswax

storage:
boxes, paper
or cloth

use by:
6 months

wrap soap
in brown
gridded paper
with pressed
flowers

gift a mix
of transparent
and opaque
soaps

Homemade wellness products

all glass has been boiled to purify

all upcycled plastic containers have been washed thoroughly

bottles, containers, atomisers and roll-ons	Essential oils, carrier oils, aloe vera, Bach flowers, vitamin E	vodka, brandy stickers, twine, pressed follage

I hate discarding the empty containers of my favourite wellness products. These days I pretty much make all the things I use in my own daily ritual. Below are some of my favourites but feel free to mix and match the scents and textures.

Roll on headache oil

20 drops of peppermint oil
2 drops of chamomile oil
2 drops of lavender oil
Pop the ball out of your empty roller and add the drops above to the roller, top up with coconut oil.

Moisture spritz

Filtered water with added vitamin E oil will cool you down in summer and hydrate your skin. Add enough filtered water to nearly fill a 200 ml (7 fl oz) container and add 3–5 drops of vitamin E, more if you feel like your skin needs it.

Packaging

I've popped a cute coloured sticker and a dried leaf or flower on each container and tied it with twine. On the bottom of each container I've written the product's name, ingredients and how to use it.

Rescue remedy

Use a small glass dropper container. Fill two-thirds with filtered water then add a bit of brandy and fill almost to the top. Now add your Bach flower remedies, these will be significant to your personality. You'll need at least 3, so make sure you have researched them before buying. Add 2 drops of each Bach flower, seal and store in the fridge for no more than a month. You'll need to take 2 drops two or three times in one day.

Hand sanitiser

Your container size will tell you what quantities you need. Place equal parts isopropyl alcohol (or vodka) and aloe vera gel in a container and stir together. Starting with 3 drops each, or more if you have a larger container, add teatree oil, cyprus oil (or eucalyptus oil) and lemon oil. Teatree oil is a wonderful antibacterial agent and blends beautifully with a citrus smell.

Face oil

Base: 2 tablespoons (1 fl oz) argan oil or jojoba oil. If possible, test to see which oil your skin prefers.

I use the below additives:

1 tablespoon rosehip oil for anti-ageing (or subsitiute with evening primrose for skin with breakouts)

4 drops of roman chamomile (for sensitve skin)

3 drops of rose geranium (for calming and anti-ageing)

Mix and pop into a small glass bottle. Your oil will keep for up to a year.

Homemade bath salts

experiment with beautiful colours and textures

130 g (4½ oz/1 cup) Epsom salts
40 g (1½ oz/⅓ cup) pink sea salt

10 g (⅓ oz/½ cup) food-safe dried rosebuds or rose petals (available at specialty tea shops)

16 g (½ oz/½ cup) green loose-leaf tea (I've used genmaicha)

A hot bath is a wonderful escape from the stresses of daily life. Magnesium sulfate, more commonly known as Epsom salts, can help soothe sore muscles and ease the tension of the day away — perfect for anyone you think could use a break!

In a bowl, combine the Epsom salts and pink sea salt. Divide the mixture into two, and add the rosebuds or petals to one half and the green loose-leaf tea to the other. Package to your liking; stamped calico drawstring bags are one of my favourite ways to gift bath salts.

You might like to replace the rosebuds or green tea with other additions, such as a couple of drops of lavender (for relaxation) or peppermint (for reinvigoration) essential oil, or skin-beautifying ingredients like powdered milk, honey or almond oil.

dried lavender is also a wonderful bath salt additive

storage: box, muslin or paper bag or cellophane

use by: 6 months

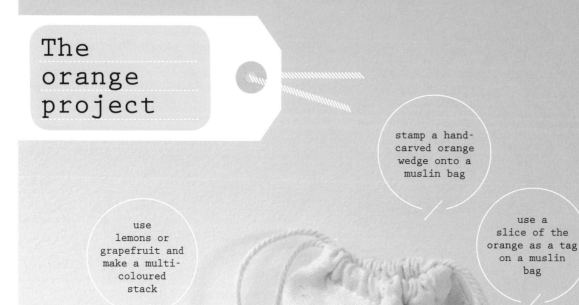

The orange project

stamp a hand-carved orange wedge onto a muslin bag

use a slice of the orange as a tag on a muslin bag

use lemons or grapefruit and make a multi-coloured stack

dip orange slices in dark chocolate for a friend with a sweet tooth

Oven-dried oranges:	Pomander ball:	a muslin bag
an orange	an orange	a stamp
sugar	cloves	linen ribbon or twine

An orange can make the perfect gift. Oven-dried oranges look beautiful in cocktails, on a dessert plate, or looped with twine on a Christmas tree. If you have patience, stud a whole orange with cloves for the most delicious-smelling gift that will perfume the whole house. If you have an orange, you can make a present.

Oven-dried orange slices

Cut one orange into fine slices.

Place in a preheated 95°C (200°F) oven on baking paper on the middle tray. Sprinkle with caster sugar and bake slowly for 2 hours or until quite dry. Check each ½ hour; you don't want them to burn.

Store in an airtight container. They will keep for up to a year.

Pomander ball

Stud an orange with cloves, making sure the cloves, are close together. You can use something to poke the holes first, or stud the cloves straight in (this is the method I use). If you keep the studded ball in a cool, dry place for a few weeks, it will dry out and keep for months or longer!

Packaging

Tie the pomander ball with a linen ribbon or some natural twine.

Tie orange slices with twine and pop into a muslin bag or glass jar.

Vegan banana and apple loaf

this loaf should keep for about a week in an airtight container

add a homemade tag, colourful baking paper and baker's twine

450 g (1 lb) bananas
1 apple (skin on or off), finely sliced
100 g (3½ oz/¾ cup) sultanas (golden raisins)
zest of 1 lemon

50 g (1¾ oz/½ cup) walnuts, roughly chopped
100 ml (3½ fl oz) vegetable oil
4–6 tablespoons almond or soy milk

75 g (2½ oz/¾ cup) rolled oats
75 g (2½ oz/½ cup) plain (all-purpose) flour
75 g (2½ oz/½ cup) self-raising flour

I love this loaf, which just so happens to be vegan and free of refined sugar. It's easy to make and is delicious for breakfast or with a cup of tea in the afternoon. When I serve this to friends, they are always astounded when I say it contains no added sugar: the fruit gives the loaf the perfect amount of sweetness. It tastes wonderful while being healthier than the average cake, and is brilliant if you're thinking of making a loved one a delicious gift. If you substitute the flour with gluten-free flour, you'll have a refined sugar-free, gluten-free, vegan treat that's difficult to beat!

Preheat your oven to 190°C (370°F).

In a large bowl, mash the bananas. Mix all of the ingredients except the flours together, until well combined. I usually do this with my hands, as I find it's quicker and more effective, though mixing with a spoon is perfectly acceptable.

Sift the flours into the bowl and carefully fold into the wet mixture with a rubber spatula or large spoon, until just combined. Take care here, as the density and texture of your cake depends on how gentle you are with your mixture: the lighter your hand when you mix, the lighter your cake.

Grease the inside of a 25 cm × 11 cm (10 in × 4¼ in) loaf (bar) tin with a little vegetable oil, then dust with plain flour until the bottom and sides of the tin are coated. Tip the excess flour out. Line the bottom of the tin with baking paper and spoon in the mixture. Bake for 40 minutes, or until a skewer inserted into the centre of the cake comes out clean. Transfer to a baking rack to cool for 10 minutes. Remove the cake from the tin and allow to cool completely on the rack. Wrap in baking paper and tie with twine.

storage: airtight tin or Tupperware

use by: 1 week

change up
the recipe
with jams,
nuts or fruits

make a variety
of biscuits to
add colour to
your gift

make
something
almost too
pretty to eat!

a wooden box
to present
biscuits can
be reused for
storage or
display

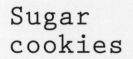

Sugar cookies

source biodegradable cellophane or party bags

HOME MADE

rolled-out dough can be layered between sheets of baking paper, double-wrapped in cling film and frozen for 4-6 weeks before thawing and baking

these biscuits are perfect sandwiched together with Nutella, lemon curd (page 70) or icing and jam

1 egg, lightly beaten 225 g (8 oz) softened butter, cubed	1 teaspoon vanilla essence 200 g (7 oz) caster (superfine) sugar	2 teaspoons baking powder 415 g (14½ oz/2¾ cups) plain (all-purpose) flour

I am completely addicted to making cut-out biscuits (or cut-out cookies, as my American friends know them). I travel to Japan regularly and never come home without a new cookie cutter. Kappabashi-dori (also known as Kitchen Street) in Tokyo is devoted to kitchenware, here you'll find cookie cutters in amazing shapes. Once you've made these biscuits you'll find so many new and interesting ways to cut and decorate them.

Preheat your oven to 200°C (390°F). Line a tray with baking paper and set aside.

In a large bowl, rub the softened butter into the sugar with your fingertips until combined, then beat with an electric mixer on medium speed until the mixture turns pale.

Add the vanilla essence to the egg and stir to combine. Beat the egg mixture into the butter mixture a little at a time; it's important to do this bit by bit so the batter doesn't curdle.

Sift the flour and baking powder into the bowl and, using a rubber spatula, fold into the wet mixture until combined. Once the dough has come together, transfer it to a lightly floured work surface and divide into two balls. Set one ball aside and flatten the other with the palm of your hand. Lightly dust your rolling pin with flour and roll out the dough until it is 5 mm (¼ in) thick. Cut the dough into shapes with your cookie cutters. Transfer the biscuits to the lined baking tray and set aside the dough scraps. Repeat with the second dough ball.

Gather up all of the dough scraps and form into a ball. Flatten with the palm of your hand, roll out with your rolling pin and cut into squares. Transfer to the baking tray – these biscuits are perfect for keeping hungry mouths and biscuit thieves at bay if you are baking for a specific occasion.

Bake the biscuits for 6–8 minutes, until the palest shade of gold. You do not want your biscuits to brown; for best results, stay close to the oven and check the biscuits' progress after 5 minutes. Transfer to a wire rack to cool completely before decorating.

The icing (frosting) and decorating stage is where you can be most creative! I often use a pre-made 'paint-style' icing product to pipe my decoration onto the biscuits – this saves on time and clean-up. You can of course whip up your own icing and pipe it with a traditional bag and a nozzle size that is right for your design.

Makes roughly
24 cookies

storage:
tins and jars

use by:
1 week

I popped them in a cardboard box with a long piece of string and she used it like a handbag!

I made Sylvie her own bag of 'Sylvie' biscuits.

As you can see, she approved!

Lemon curd

sandwich sugar cookies (page 66) with lemon curd

include lemons from your garden with your present

| 3 eggs | juice and zest of 2½ lemons |
| 100 g (3½ oz) unsalted butter | 150 g (5½ oz) sugar |

My husband Steve and I planted lemon trees in our tiny courtyard. Every year there is an abundance of lemons that we love to give to friends and family to use. Steve is a pretty impressive pastry cook and loves to make jars of curd from the lemons in our garden. In fact, this is our most favourite dessert! When we got married, we chose the venue for a small party based on the chef's lemon tart (which we had in lieu of a wedding cake). I always think that when something is made especially for you, it tastes ten times better than when you make it yourself. When it's not dolloped into mini pastries, we like to dunk Italian savoiardi into it.

In a bowl, lightly whisk the eggs and pass through a fine mesh strainer to remove any lumps.

Combine the butter, lemon juice, zest and sugar in a saucepan over low heat. Stir until all of the butter has melted and the sugar has dissolved, then remove from the heat. Reduce the heat to very low.

Whisk the eggs into the butter mixture and return the saucepan to the heat, whisking constantly until the curd thickens. Do not allow it to come to a boil; this will curdle the mixture. Remove the saucepan from the heat once more and pour the curd into sterilised jars.

For a variation on this simple recipe, simply substitute any other citrus fruit for the lemons (taking amounts into account, of course). Blood orange curd and ruby red grapefruit curd are two of my favourites.

If you have a lemon tree, press some lemon flowers to go with your gift

storage: glass jars

use by: 2 weeks

Chocolate truffles

add the seeds of a vanilla bean to the cream for vanilla-scented truffles

roll white-chocolate truffles in crumbled freeze-dried raspberries

HOME MADE

add a dash of liqueur to the cream for grown-up truffles

add grated orange zest to the ganache for a choc-orange flavour

250 g (9 oz) high-quality dark chocolate, chopped
170 ml (5½ fl oz/⅔ cup) cream (35% fat content or greater)

1 tablespoon glucose syrup, light corn syrup or mild honey
20 g (¾ oz) unsalted butter, at room temperature

good-quality unsweetened cocoa, for rolling

Homemade chocolate truffles are such an impressive gift even if they are super-simple to make! While this recipe uses dark chocolate for the base and cocoa for rolling, you can also substitute milk or white chocolate and decorate however you please — crushed toasted hazelnuts for milk chocolate or chopped pistachios for white chocalate are some of my favourites. These truffles do melt easily, so they are best hand-delivered!

Place the chopped chocolate in a large, heatproof bowl.

In a small saucepan over low heat, bring the cream and glucose syrup to a simmer. Remove from the heat and pour over the chopped chocolate. Allow to stand for 15 seconds, then, with a rubber spatula or wooden spoon, carefully incorporate the hot cream and chocolate to make a ganache. Add the butter and stir through the ganache

until it is completely dissolved and the ganache is smooth and glossy.

Cover the bowl with cling film and place in the refrigerator for 10–20 minutes, or until the ganache is partly set and able to be rolled into balls. Remove from the refrigerator and, using a teaspoon, scoop out balls of ganache and place on a tray covered with baking paper. Alternatively, you can

transfer the ganache to a piping bag and pipe balls directly onto the tray. Place the tray in the refrigerator to allow the ganache balls to harden up.

To decorate, sift the cocoa onto a plate and, working quickly so the chocolate doesn't melt and stick to your hands, roll the ganache balls in the cocoa to make rustic truffles. Store in the refrigerator until you are ready to package them up.

make sure you buy good-quality ingredients for this recipe

storage: biodegradable cellophane bags or a tin

use by: 1 month

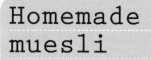

Homemade muesli

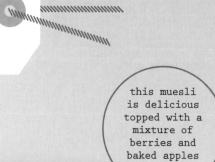

this muesli
is delicious
topped with a
mixture of
berries and
baked apples
or pears

100 g (3½ oz/1 cup) rolled oats
40 g (1½ oz/⅓ cup) slivered almonds

40 g (1½ oz/⅓ cup) sultanas or dried cranberries, or a mix of both

30 g (1 oz/¼ cup) goji berries
4 dried pear halves, diced

A good breakfast is a great start to the day, especially if it has been made and delivered with love. You can play around with the dried fruits and nuts in this recipe - toasted hazelnuts, sunflower seeds and sesame seeds are all delicious, or omit nuts completely if your recipient is allergic - and a teeny amount of cinnamon, if desired, is a surefire way to spice things up!

Combine all ingredients in a bowl and package to your liking.

For a decadent toasted variation, heat 1 tablespoon each of honey, brown sugar and rice bran oil in a small saucepan. Stir until the sugar has dissolved, then pour over the combined ingredients. Mix well, spread on a lined baking tray and bake in a preheated 150°C (300°F) oven, stirring every 10 minutes, until golden brown. Allow to cool completely before packaging.

this delicious muesli is gluten-free!

storage:
glass jars

use by:
1 week

Handmade tea bags

I love rose tea and Turkish delight together

try using vintage stamps with an unusual design

a pencil and pinking shears	good-quality loose leaf tea	uncoloured natural twine
loose-weave muslin (cheesecloth)	(I've used rose tea)	vintage postal stamps

A cup of hot tea in a favourite chair is one of the simplest stress-relievers one could possibly ask for. These homemade tea bags can be customised to suit anyone's taste in tea, and a parcel containing these personalised infusions is like a delivery of peace and tranquility.

Using a pencil, draw circles approximately 16 cm (6¼ in) in diameter onto the muslin (I used an overturned breakfast bowl as a template). Using pinking shears, cut out the circles. Place a small amount of tea (about 1 teaspoon, see example opposite, or use the recommended amount for one cup according to the packet) into the centre of each muslin circle.

For each circle, gather up the edges into the centre and bunch into a neat shape. Tie with twine to secure the tea, leaving enough twine to drape over the edge of a cup and for you to attach the postage stamp labels. Choose two matching stamps and sandwich the twine between them. And there you have it! Perfectly pretty handmade tea bags, just right for any tea-loving friend.

storage:
tins and jars

use by:
6 months

Garden fresh herb tea

chamomile flowers, tiny roses, the list is endless when it comes to herbal teas

fresh mint or spearmint from the garden steeped in hot water makes a delicious tea

pop a tiny amount
of beetroot juice
into your sugar
cookies for pink
cookies (page 66)

press flowers
into iced
sugar cookies
(page 66)

chocolate mint is
also a delicous
mint variety to
steep in
hot water

Dried-flower wreath

wreaths in
different sizes
look beautiful
styled together
on a wall

this wreath
can also make a
beautiful statement
on a brown paper
package tied up
with string

| a wooden embroidery hoop (the size should suit your foliage) | dried flowers and/or leaves (I used Australian natives) | a hooked clip
a cute hanger (I used a circular coathanger) |

I love drying flowers. If I see beautiful flowers to forage in the wild, or am gifted a bunch of flowers, they will soon be hanging upside-down somewhere in my house then art-directed into small spaces around treasured things. This simple wreath is the perfect gift for a like-minded nature lover.

Select the nicest dried flowers and/or leaves from your collection.

Start to arrange around the smaller hoop making sure most of the flower and leaf action is away from the placement of the second hoop.

Now add a second layer. I chose to lay my flowers first and then my leaves.

Unscrew the top hoop so it is as wide as it can get and carefully place over your bottom hoop. Some foliage may come loose or break, don't worry, you just want to capture as much as you can.

Tighten the screw a little and start filling the gaps with extra foliage until you are happy. Then completely tighten the screw.

Now you have the gift of nature's everlasting beauty in a pure circle. Wrap in a soft muslin bag or calico and tie with another piece of foliage. Beautiful.

Seeds and seedlings

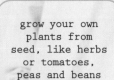

grow your own
plants from
seed, like herbs
or tomatoes,
peas and beans

self collected
seeds are also
a lovely gift

Seeds

seeds from wet fruit and vegetables like tomato, and cucumber	dry seeds from seed pods like beans and peas	a paper bag envelopes an airtight container

Gifting seeds from your own veggie patch is a lovely way to share, and friends to start growing their own food. You can also get crafty with the presentation of your seeds, and why not include a favourite recipe in with your gift. Design up handmade origami envelopes or make a rubber stamp (see page 29) with a simple illustration of the grown fruit.

Wet seeds

Scoop out seeds from ripened fruit and place in a jar of water for a few days. By this time the seeds will have unattached themselves from their surrounding pulp. Discard the water and rinse the seeds. To dry, spread the seeds out on brown paper. When seeds are FULLY dry, store as per column 3.

Dry seeds

Collect pea and bean pods when they have started to wither and turn brown and the seeds are already dried in the pod. Take out the seeds and dry them, spread out on brown paper in a cool dry spot for 2 weeks (until completely hard). Store as per column 3 instructions.

Avoid moisture at all costs

Moisture is the enemy of your seeds; they should be fully dry before you store them in paper envelopes and then in an airtight container.

Spread out your seeds

It's extremely important to spread out your seeds whilst drying.

Soak an avocado pip in warm water overnight. Then dry the pip for 2 days. Put 4 toothpicks in the middle of the seed and with the thinner side up balance over a glass cup filled with water (the rounder side of the pip dipping into the water). A root system should push through the seed in 2-6 weeks.

Upcycled
tomato
tins

| tomato tins or any lovely tins you have in your house | basil seedlings or other herbs or plants of your choice | potting mix small pebbles |

It's no secret that I love collecting tins of any kind. A favourite thing I do in any overseas country is go to the supermarket and buy beautifully packaged utilitarian products. Tins are a great way to plant seedlings or any kind of small plant. I love to make a parcel of basil seedlings that I have popped into egg cartons, a tin of tomatoes, dried chickpeas or lentils, pasta or rice and a recipe to use them all in a one pot dinner, then add a note on how to use the tin to repot the seedlings.

After using the contents of your tins, wash them out.

Put a small layer of pebbles at the bottom of each tin for drainage then add potting mix.

Add your seedling or plant and water in.

I sometimes like to add a layer of sphagnum moss to the top of each tin as it retains so much water. If you make the kokedama on page 88 you'll have plenty of sphagnum moss left over.

Plant herbs you would use ever week and arrange on a windowsill and water often.

If you would like to gift a dinner package, add the instructions on how to pot the seedlings and the recipe to the pack.

This is a vegan recipe but you can add parmesan (if you use pasta) or a scoop of greek yoghurt and/or grilled haloumi (if you use rice).

You'll need a cute teatowel to furoshiki all the ingredients. I have also used a box and calico and natural bags. Pack dried chickpeas or lentils, wholemeal pasta or rice and a tin of tomatoes.

Gift the basil seedlings separately in an egg carton.

Recipe

Soak dried chickpeas overnight, then boil in water for 40 minutes or until soft.

Take one cup of cooked chickpeas, one tin of tomatoes, one cup of rice or wholemeal pasta, ½ a stock cube and 2 cups of water and bring all to the boil. Boil for about 20 minutes, adding water if it is too dry. By this stage it should look like a risotto or a cooked pasta dish consistency.

When done, add basil, salt and pepper and parmesan if you are not vegan.

Roasted tomato sauce

on the label or tag, give your friend some serving suggestions for the sauce

10 roma (plum) tomatoes, halved lengthways olive oil, for drizzling	balsamic vinegar, for drizzling 3 garlic cloves, unpeeled	5 basil leaves, torn in two, plus extra whole leaves for bottling

When my friend May was pregnant, I would sometimes leave a fresh jar of this delicious sauce on her doorstep as a quick dinner solution. It's technically a pasta sauce, but half an hour after I had dropped it off at May's, she would message me to say she had eaten it warm, straight out of the jar! So, while this tomato sauce is perfect for pasta, or for adding to a tin of beans to make fancy baked beans (which I love dolloped on toast with a little parmesan), don't let that limit your serving suggestions. Did I mention it's vegan, too?

Preheat your oven to 160°C (320°F). Pop your tomato halves into a lined baking dish and season well with salt and pepper. Pour a generous glug of olive oil over each tomato, then follow suit with about one-third of the amount of balsamic. Mix the tomatoes, oil and vinegar together with your hands, then add the garlic cloves and top each tomato half with a basil leaf half. Roast for an hour, checking every 20 minutes and rotating the dish to ensure even cooking, if necessary. Remove from the oven and allow to cool.

When the tomatoes have cooled, spoon into a clean glass jar (or jars), adding a few extra basil leaves to the sauce, preferably where they can be seen. Fasten the lid and have fun decorating the jar, or make a label or tag. This will last up to a week in a refrigerator – if it isn't eaten before then!

Serves 2 as a pasta sauce for dinner

use as a condiment to go with your favourite dish

storage:
glass jars

use by:
1 week

Japanese moss ball (Kokedama)

as an option use twine to wrap a layer of baby's tears or foraged moss to the peat moss outer layer

peat moss, sphagnum moss and bonsai soil come in store-bought bags so you'll need a bag of each

peat moss sphagnum moss bonsai soil mix twine	scissors mini fern or other small houseplant water	3 bowls (about 2 cm/¾ in diameter) optional: baby's tears or foraged moss

Koke means moss in Japanese, and these artfully made moss balls can be spotted in stylish shops, ryokans and sometimes as part of a plant display out the front of residential houses. I've long admired delicate plants gently emerging from these beautiful mossy spheres. Making a kokedama is very therapeutic. With practice you will master this art, but remember nature is imperfect and any creation you make will be beautiful.

 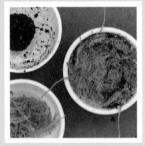 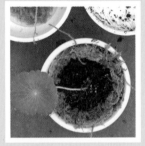

Mix ½ cup of both peat moss and bonsai soil in a small bowl, add ¼ cup water and make a soil ball in your hands; add a bit more water if needed. You should have a perfectly rounded ball. Set aside.

Half fill a second bowl with water and add a handful of sphagnum moss. Swish it around in the water until it plumps up. Cut two 40 mm (1½ in) pieces of twine and lay over a third bowl like a cross. Press a 2–3 cm (¾–1 in) thickness of sphagnum moss into the bowl, as if you were lining it with pastry, making sure there are no holes.

Place the soil ball in the middle of the bowl lined with sphagnum moss. Take your fern out of its pot and shake off the soil so you can see the roots. Make a hole in the top of your soil ball and plant your fern. Don't worry if your ball falls apart a little; you can press it back into the circular shape once the fern has been added.

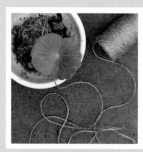

Carefully lift up the sides of the sphagnum moss and press it around the ball. Do this bit by bit. When the exterior moss is covering the top of the soil ball sufficiently take one piece of twine and tie firmly at the top of the ball next to the fern, then do the same with the other piece of twine.

Carefully lift everything out of the bowl and press in the sphagnum moss by cupping your hands, trying to make a circular shape. Unravel a long piece of twine (do not cut), place the top of the twine at the top of your ball and start to wind the twine around the ball. You can wind in whatever pattern you like; I wind mine in a beach ball type pattern (I don't wind horizontally, only vertically. Keep cupping the ball into shape with your hands but please remember, whatever shape your kokedama is – it will look beautiful. Imperfect can be perfect with this project. With your final wind, loop the twine under one of the wrapped pieces of twine for strength, then tie a knot. If you want to hang the kokedama, leave a long piece of twine after the knot to tie and hang with.

You'll have enough soil for multiple kokedama and I guarantee as you get the hang of this project, your moss balls will become more perfect and you'll feel confident to try new plants, different twine and slightly different shapes. I love to make kokedama without a plant and, after I've wrapped the ball in twine, forage baby's tears in my garden and cover the ball with it. I then add another layer of twine.

Water the kokedama by popping it in a bowl of water for 20 minutes every week, squeezing out excess water and spritzing or misting between soaks if the weather is warm or you have heating on.

Here I have made three varieties. A baby's tears option, a pennywort option (see the plant shown in the steps) and a fern option.

Display on a plate, or hang in the bathroom or any room in the house.

Makes 1 kokedama

Growing & foraging flowers

Beautiful flowers can easily be grown from seeds or seedlings or foraged on walks in your local area. The gift of flowers is a beautiful gesture that can also be extended by pressing the treasured petals and leaves or hanging the bunch upside down to dry and display.

wrap flowers with pretty homemade papers cut with pinking shears

nature has its own unbeatable colour palette

my friend Kate
knitted these
woollen socks
for me

Kintsugi
hack

powdered pigments in gold or silver ceramic glue	a paint brush an upcycled plastic container	an icypole stick (for mixing glue and powdered pigment)

The art of kintsugi (repairing with gold) is a Japanese craft like no other. It takes a broken porcelain or ceramic piece and puts it back together in a pure art form that can make it more beautiful and valuable than the original. The piece shows the scars of life, something to be treasured, not to be thrown away. Traditional techniques take years to master. The following is a hack for putting your broken things back together with beauty and thought.

Arrange your broken thing the way it will be pieced back together.

In a plastic container add a small blob of ceramic glue. Sprinkle in a touch of pigment and mix with an icypole stick (a little goes a long way).

Carefully paint a small amount of glue on one broken side, join the matching side and hold together for about ten minutes. If you find your glue has gone a bit blobby, wait for your piece to dry, then using a blade or scalpel cut off the unwanted bits.

Move onto the next part of the piece. You will need to keep making small batches of pigment glue for each piece as the glue dries quickly.

When your piece is back together, you can then run a tiny bit of glue and pigment over the cracks on the finished plate.

Carefully paint along the cracks with a thin layer of glue and sprinkle over some of the pigment. Dust on with another paint brush or massage into the filled cracks with your fingers.

It may take a bit of practise to get your glue the thickness you like so you may want to practice on something basic first before you try on a precious piece.

Essentially you are gluing your piece back together so take care with the amount of glue you use and the lines you create.

Remember, imperfect is perfect.

Half the fun of sustainable gifting comes from the making and decoration of the box and its contents. There are lots of different creative decisions to be made, so sit down, have a cup of tea and sketch out your designs first – a good idea for any creative endeavour! Choose a theme and a colour combination, then make a list of the materials you think you'll need. Make sure your packaging is strong enough for its contents, and think about whether you can reuse something you already have in your house: cloth packaging, glass jars, decorated upcyled packing materials. The possibilities are endless. The following pages are designed to spark your imagination and help you style your gifts with creativity and imagination.

Thinking
outside the box

Equipment

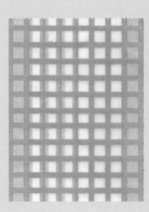

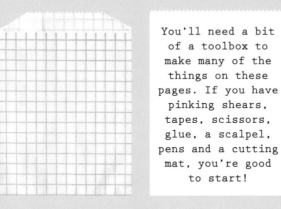
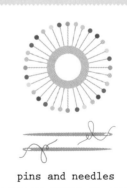

You'll need a bit of a toolbox to make many of the things on these pages. If you have pinking shears, tapes, scissors, glue, a scalpel, pens and a cutting mat, you're good to start!

pins and needles

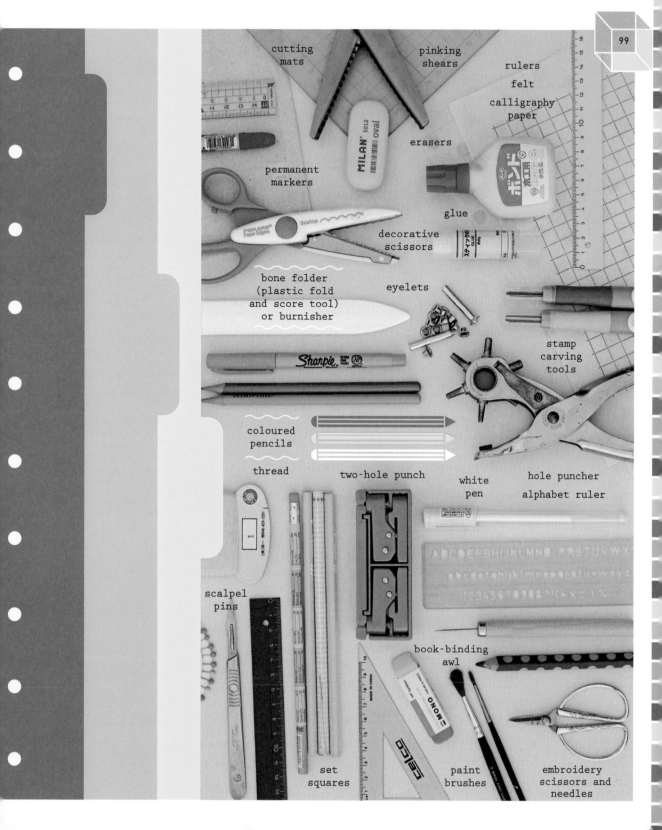

cutting mats

pinking shears

rulers

felt

calligraphy paper

erasers

permanent markers

glue

decorative scissors

bone folder (plastic fold and score tool) or burnisher

eyelets

stamp carving tools

coloured pencils

thread

two-hole punch

white pen

hole puncher

alphabet ruler

scalpel

pins

book-binding awl

set squares

paint brushes

embroidery scissors and needles

Colour & pattern ideas

When I start planning a parcel, like a box to put a gift in, the first thing I do is think about building a colour palette and pattern ideas. For instance, if it's a present for a mother and baby I'd focus on a pastel palette with a cute motif.

Here are some of my favourite palettes and patterns to use as a starting point for your creativity. I love to bring together lots of recycled papers and fabrics, strings, ribbons and stamped papers to make a beautiful package.

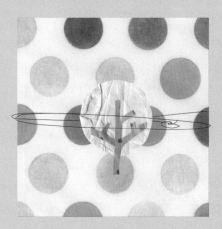

Boxes

MAKE YOUR OWN BOX

Making your own box allows you to have fun with your own creativity; you can personalise every part of your package, both inside and out.

On pages 153–157, you will find a number of templates ready to be photocopied and transferred to the paper or card of your choice, but you can dismantle any box you like and create your own template by tracing its edges and marking the folds.

Before you choose the paper or card to make your box from, think about what you will be including in your package, as the box needs to be sturdy enough to accommodate the contents. You might need to practise constructing your box from a few different thicknesses of paper or card to make sure your box will be a suitable strength; if you're worried about waste, you can always test your materials by building small, rather than full-size, versions of your box. Then you can use these for a tiny package!

If you want to go the extra mile with your custom-built box, you can line it with fun coloured or patterned paper. Just make sure that you line the inside of the box before you assemble it, while it is still flat, as it's much easier to do it this way.

Remember, the heavier the card or paper stock you use, the firmer you'll need to be with your folds. Scoring along the folded edges with the back of your scalpel or craft knife, or with a proper paper scorer or folding bone, is the best way to get lovely crisp folds and a neat finish.

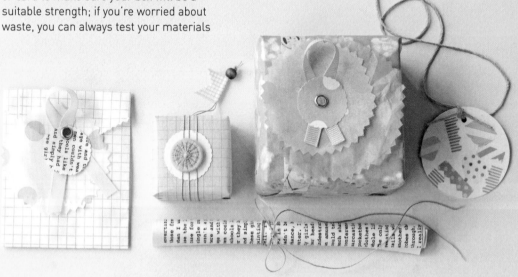

Boxes

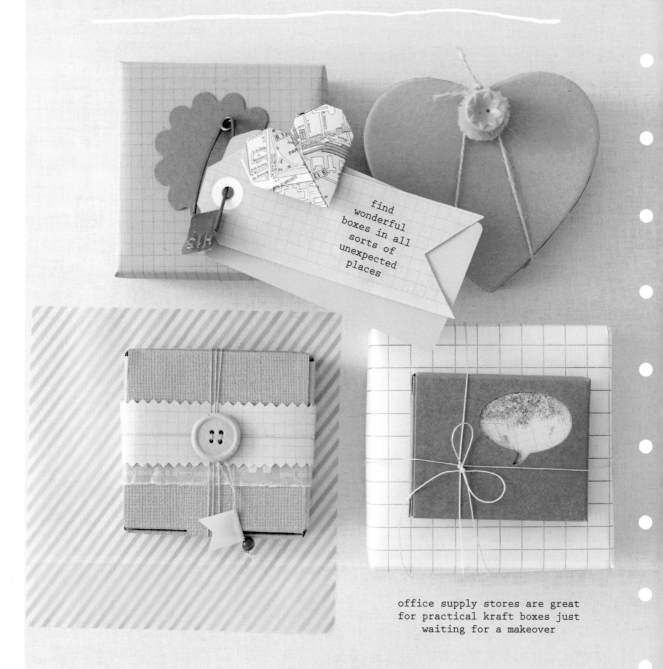

find wonderful boxes in all sorts of unexpected places

office supply stores are great for practical kraft boxes just waiting for a makeover

PRETTY UP A BROWN KRAFT BOX

With a natural kraft base, try...

using a simple, palette of white or black

using vintage magazines for collages

using just one bright colour

covering your box with vintage stamps

a bright ribbon and homemade name tag

tying with natural string and attaching an origami heart (page 25) or fresh flowers, leaves or feathers

look for reusable boxes from packaging around things you buy; you may be surprised by what you find

Boxes

wrap tiny
boxes with
love and
care

mix up box
sizes and
shapes

a pop of colour makes the box so modern!

one perfect dried flower looks exquisite

Origami

THE JAPANESE ART OF PAPER FOLDING

The art of origami can be traced back to the early years of Japan's Edo period (1603–1868). Origami models can be beautifully simple or very complex, and are often made to be given to friends and family, as well as being used to beautify parcels. Many origami items start from a square paper base; for visual effect, many papers have a two-sided design. Origami paper is usually sold in inexpensive packs of 20 or more, and is available in art and craft stores, but any paper will do.

If you find yourself with a rainy day to while away, I highly recommend spending some time learning a few paper-folding techniques. I have included several in the pages of this book, but the internet is a treasure trove of tutorials.

Origami items are a lovely addition to the top of a package, or a charming surprise tucked inside one (see origami heart, page 25), but you can also go all out and make a box out of origami (see opposite), too. Folding a special message into shapes is also cute.

The biggest tip to origami success is to take your time and fold your corners perfectly. Look into buying a bone folder if you want your folds to be extra-crisp. Origami models look extremely impressive for a minimal amount of work, especially once you have mastered the basic techniques and shapes. You will not regret making origami for gifting – in fact, you'll want to add a piece to every future present you make.

look at an online tutorial if you need a extra help

origami boxes can be made to any size

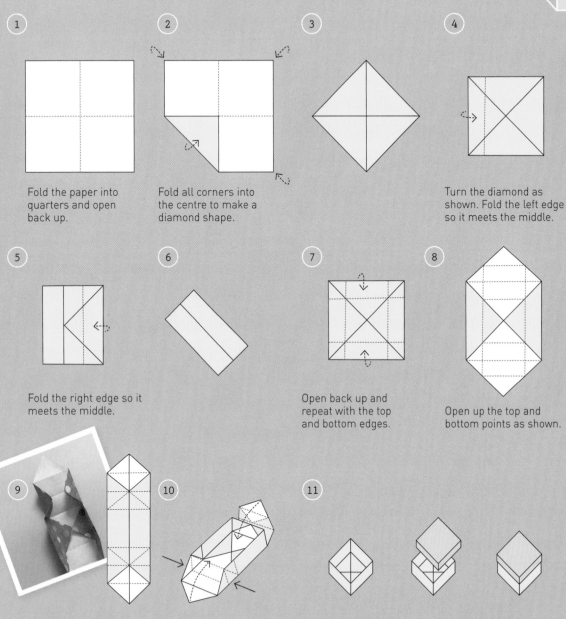

1

Fold the paper into quarters and open back up.

2

Fold all corners into the centre to make a diamond shape.

3

4

Turn the diamond as shown. Fold the left edge so it meets the middle.

5

Fold the right edge so it meets the middle.

6

7

Open back up and repeat with the top and bottom edges.

8

Open up the top and bottom points as shown.

9

Fold the left and right edges along the crease so they form the first two walls of the box.

10

Pinch and fold the creases shown and bring up the remaining two walls. Fold the remaining paper into the bottom of the box.

11

Congratulations, the body of the box is made! To make the box lid, follow the same instructions, but make the top a little bigger and the walls a little shorter. To do this, once you reach step 4, place the body of the box in the centre of the lid paper and fold the edges around the box. This way, you know the lid walls will fall outside the box body walls, as the lid top will be larger.

Boxes

"Try a
random
act of
kindness."

Preloved containers

draw faces and add tiny sticker cheeks to the eggs

if you have chickens, fresh eggs make a fantastic gift

craft with papers, twine and tags

TAKEAWAY FOOD CONTAINERS

It may seem like a funny suggestion, but takeaway food packaging has become smarter and, in some cases, more attractive over the years. Unused cardboard takeaway containers with handles – the kind you might get from your local Chinese restaurant – make great containers for gifts. You can even dress up a polystyrene container with a cute paper bellyband. Don't discount the humble takeaway box; you'll find that, with a bit of love, these utilitarian containers can become super-stylish and surprisingly pretty with a few thoughtful additions.

PRELOVED BOXES

I'm not sure if it is because I am a graphic designer, or if it's just a thing that some people do, but I love to keep – or, dare I say it, to hoard – pretty boxes and packaging that has housed things I have bought. I've always loved hermit crabs, too, so maybe it's the idea of giving something old a new purpose, rather than throwing it away, that I appreciate.

Preloved boxes are wonderful for parcels, since you are reusing something that would otherwise be pulped or go to landfill – not to mention it won't cost you anything. Try collecting and saving shoeboxes, garment boxes, soapboxes, vintage board game boxes (if you've lost half the pieces), perfume boxes, wooden wine boxes, hat boxes, old suitcases and school cases, and any nicely shaped cardboard box that you've come across. If you have a friend who, for instance, loves to buy shoes or has expensive tastes in wine but always throws out the boxes, ask if she wouldn't mind passing any particularly beautiful boxes on to you. My mum is always bringing me things that she thinks I can make use of – and most of the time I can!

Jars & bottles

VINTAGE FINDS

Thrift stores are the perfect place to hunt for vintage jars and bottles. There are so many wonderful shapes and designs to scout for!

If the lids on any of the jars you find are a little corroded, you can still package non-edibles in them, disguising the rust with a piece of fabric secured with an elastic band and finished off with a pretty ribbon. Don't be dismayed if you are looking to package pickles, jams or spreads in vintage jars with corroded or missing lids: many vintage jars were produced in standard sizes that still exist today, and your local canning and preserving supply store may carry lids that fit.

Vintage bottles are ideal for homemade tomato sauce (see page 86) or homemade lemonade. If you brew your own beer, why not bottle it in some vintage flip-top bottles (replacement rubber seals are easy to pick up online) to provide an artisan theme?

STORE-BOUGHT ALTERNATIVES

There is a fantastic selection of inexpensive glass jars and bottles to be found in stores, especially culinary supply stores or canning and preserving specialists, where you can choose from the largest pickling jar to the tiniest jam jar, from practical metal or plastic screw-top lids to pretty glass and cork lids.

What you fill the jar with, as well as the jar you choose, will depend on how you are delivering your package. If you are sending it via post, you should opt for plastic jars to avoid breakages. However, there is a downside to plastic jars: you can't sterilise them properly, which rules out using them for jams, preserves or pickles. If your heart is set on sending preserves in the mail, several small glass jars packaged very well with bubble wrap are much more likely to survive the post than one big one. Whether you're using plastic or glass, make sure you choose an option with a sturdy screw-top lid to avoid a spilling or spoiling disaster!

Packaging food

pastels, spots, grids, natural fabric and twine make for a pretty offering

vegan banana and apple loaf recipe (see page 62)

glue
vintage
papers
onto
your
bags

make origami
hearts (page XX)

make
your
own
tags

use
washi
tape on
your
box

wrap
chocolate
truffles
in baking
paper

make a tag to match
your bag

decorate the inside
of your box

line with cute
wax paper

this is an upcycled
see-through box

wrap sweets in a tube

Tins

I still have a tin that was given to me when I was a little girl. I had felt left out at a family party, where most of the kids were a little older than me. A family friend, Brian, went and bought me a tin of Mackintosh chocolates so I could share with the group. In no time, I had forgotten my worries and was happily playing along with the rest of the kids. Looking back, I realise this was my first saved tin. Brian's act of kindness really resonated with me, hence why I still have the tin to this day. It may look vintage now, but originally it was bright, shiny and new, a segue to happiness.

VINTAGE FINDS

I love to collect vintage tins. I am always on the lookout for them online or at flea markets, and I especially love mid-century designs. Old tins may not be appropriate to house edible goods, but they are fantastic for just about anything else:.

STORE-BOUGHT ALTERNATIVES

I've been known to buy items just for the tin. Toffee tins and tea and biscuit tins are the best for storing my ever-growing collection of ephemera! A store-bought tin is great for packaging homemade sweet treats and baked goods – I find they really hold the freshness in. If you are lucky enough to find a great-looking new tin, with a design you love, why not buy a couple? Keep one for yourself and use the other for your parcel.

all these
cans and tins
can be reused

try using
cute drink
cans as vases

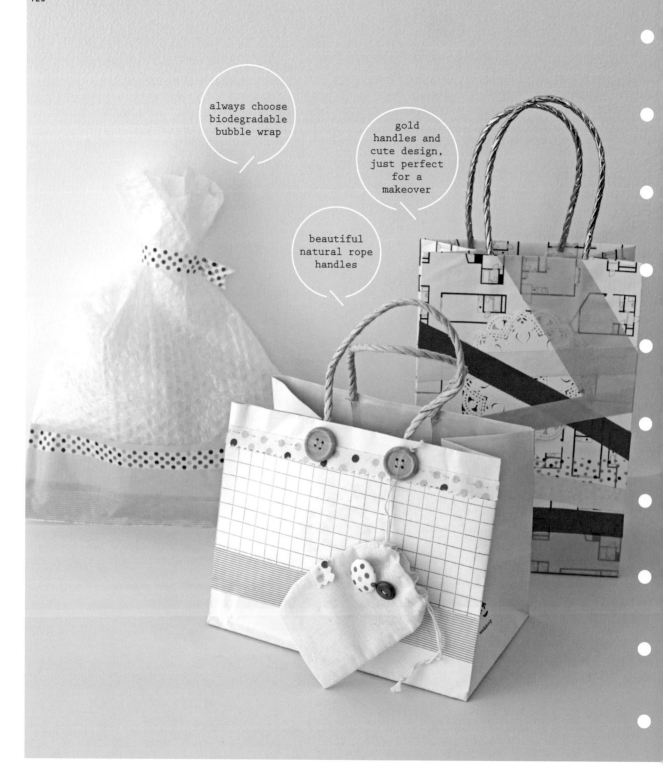

Bags

CALICO BAGS

Fabric bags are great for gifts, especially if you are including food in your parcel. A fresh baguette popping out of the top of a fabric-stamped calico bag is an adorable sight! You can tie the handles together with a ribbon or sew a button onto the front and attach some looped twine onto the back, or add a bright fabric pocket to the front to carry your handmade card. If you have an old shirt that you are going to dissect for scraps, unpick the pocket and add it to your bag.

You can liven up a plain calico bag by stamping a bold repetitive pattern all over (see page 30 for inspiration). Make sure you use fabric stamp pads, and wash your stamped bag before using (especially if you are including food in your bag). You are also gifting a reusable item, so think about the recipient's personality, aesthetic and favourite colours before adding your pocket or fabric stamping. See pages 29–31 for more on how to stamp, including design ideas and templates.

UPCYCLED BAGS

I am a bit of a hoarder when it comes to well-designed retail bags. I have a large collection at home, made up mostly of interesting bags from overseas holidays and my favourite local deli and provisions stores. If a bag is made out of beautiful paper, has cute handles or an interesting design, I like to personalise it and turn it into a brand new version of itself. Buttons, washi tape, a bit of watercolour, stitched fabric or anything else that takes my fancy may be added to the original design. I love to use these bags to house gifts. You can decorate a bag from a fashionable store or give your loved one a bag they have never seen before, with embellishments that suit their style. And it's great for the environment!

MAKING A SUSTAINABLE BUBBLE WRAP BAG

If you really need to wrap your present with care, you can buy wonderful biodegradable bubble wrap from office supply stores. With a little ingenuity, you can create a cute pouch or drawstring bag to house the precious item. Thank goodness for green technology!

Bags

PAPER

I love to collect vintage Japanese packaging; whenever I am in Tokyo, my friend Shoko takes me to stores that have special sections for packaging from the Showa Era – my favourite period for packaging design. When in Japan, I save and bring home paper boxes, wrapping and shopping bags. Even if it is a simple white or one-colour bag, I'll snip off the handles and replace them with ribbons, or make my own paper handles, then I'll add tags or stickers over the shop logo or decorate the bag in some other way that gives it a whole new lease on life.

I am also a huge fan of wax-paper bags; I just think they are so beautiful. Kitchen bags, sweet bags, polka-dot plastic bags: all make wonderful packaging for gifts. Everyday things can be made extraordinary with a little bit of ingenious thinking.

start
your vintage
packaging
collection
today!

add homemade
tags to
vintage bags

the muslin
bag below is
full of hiba
woodchips.
I hang this
in my closet
to keep away
moths. You
can also fill
natural bags
with cedar
balls

Bags

Calico, linen and organic-cotton bags are a favourite of mine to use for any and all projects. From soap to food they house everything beautifully and can be used and reused for years to come. Making your own bags out of upcycled clothing is also fun, especially if you find a vintage fabric on a shirt or dress that's too big or too small for you in the local charity shop.

Natural fibres make for the best bags; tie them with string or linen ribbons, or add buttons for interest.

If you are a fan of colour, add splashes with a selection of ribbons, stamp bright shapes or stitch something bold onto the natural canvas.

Make a potato stamp and print a leaf onto the fabric, or paint it on. Dried leaves match natural bags beautifully.

ECO FABRICS:

calico

linen

jute

organic cotton

bamboo

hemp

silk

also new fabrics like:

rPET

SeaCell

Lyocell

soy fabrics

Drawstring bags

stamp something pretty (see page 29) onto calico bags

stripes and neutrals with pops of colour are pretty

add buttons to the drawstring

decorate with
recycled paper
and pretty
labels

make fabric
bags to pop
presents in

Bags for food

Packaging food in fun colourful bags has such a nostalgic childhood feeling.

I love making a bag each for friends and including something different for each person.

Include chocolate liqueurs for a grown-up party feel, or a sweet that holds a family or school memory.

Make sure you are on top of your friends' gluten-free, vegan, nut-free requirements.

IDEAS FOR INCLUSIONS

oven-dried citrus (page 61)

chocolate truffles (page 72)

dried fruit and nut balls

roasted or candied nuts

biscuits (page 66)

chocolates in cute shapes

fruit cake

rice crakers

chocolate disks with almonds

chocolate-coated nuts and sultanas

toffee-apple pieces

matcha shortbread

kompeto (Japanese hard candy)

chocolate liqueurs

Sustainable gifting is infinitely customisable for just about any person or occasion – but the sheer number of possibilities can be a little overwhelming! Do you make something simple and from the heart, or do you opt for the over-the-top, super-charming option? How your gift will be delivered, the reason you are sending it, how much time you have, and the kind of person your recipient is will all contribute to the kind of package you make. Don't stress if you're working with a tiny budget or scant free time. Limitations often give rise to our greatest creative moments!

In this chapter, you'll find a list of my favourite package themes to help you put together something special for your loved one. If you can't find one that's just right for the occasion, why not mix and match components? The possibilities are endless.

The
complete
package

Wrapping

FUROSHIKI: SQUARE WRAPPING
Furoshiki are a special kind of cloth used to wrap items in Japan. Traditionally, furoshiki were used to wrap and transport clothing and produce, but in more recent times they have been used to decorate gifts.

Thanks to the flexible nature of the cloth, you can wrap just about any shape or size, so long as you select a fabric square big enough to wrap your parcel. Books look beautiful wrapped in furoshiki (see page 135), and even odd shapes can be wrapped furoshiki-style.

My favourite way to use furoshiki is to choose a beautiful scarf and have it double as wrapping for the complete package.

TENUGUI: RECTANGULAR WRAPPING
A tenugui is a long piece of cotton cloth (around 35 cm x 90 cm or 14 in x 35½ in in size) that is traditionally used in Japan as a headband, as a souvenir, or to wrap bottles and other long gifts. I buy tenugui to use as table runners and to beautify surfaces, as there are always so many beautiful patterns to choose from. Sake or wine looks beautiful wrapped in tenugui (see below and page 134), and is a perfect addition to a gift, as the beautiful cloth can be reused or repurposed.

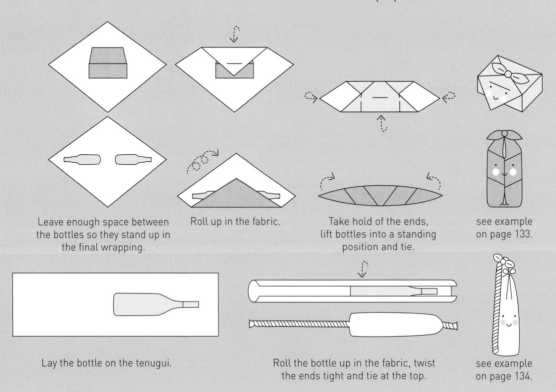

Leave enough space between the bottles so they stand up in the final wrapping.

Roll up in the fabric.

Take hold of the ends, lift bottles into a standing position and tie.

see example on page 133.

Lay the bottle on the tenugui.

Roll the bottle up in the fabric, twist the ends tight and tie at the top.

see example on page 134.

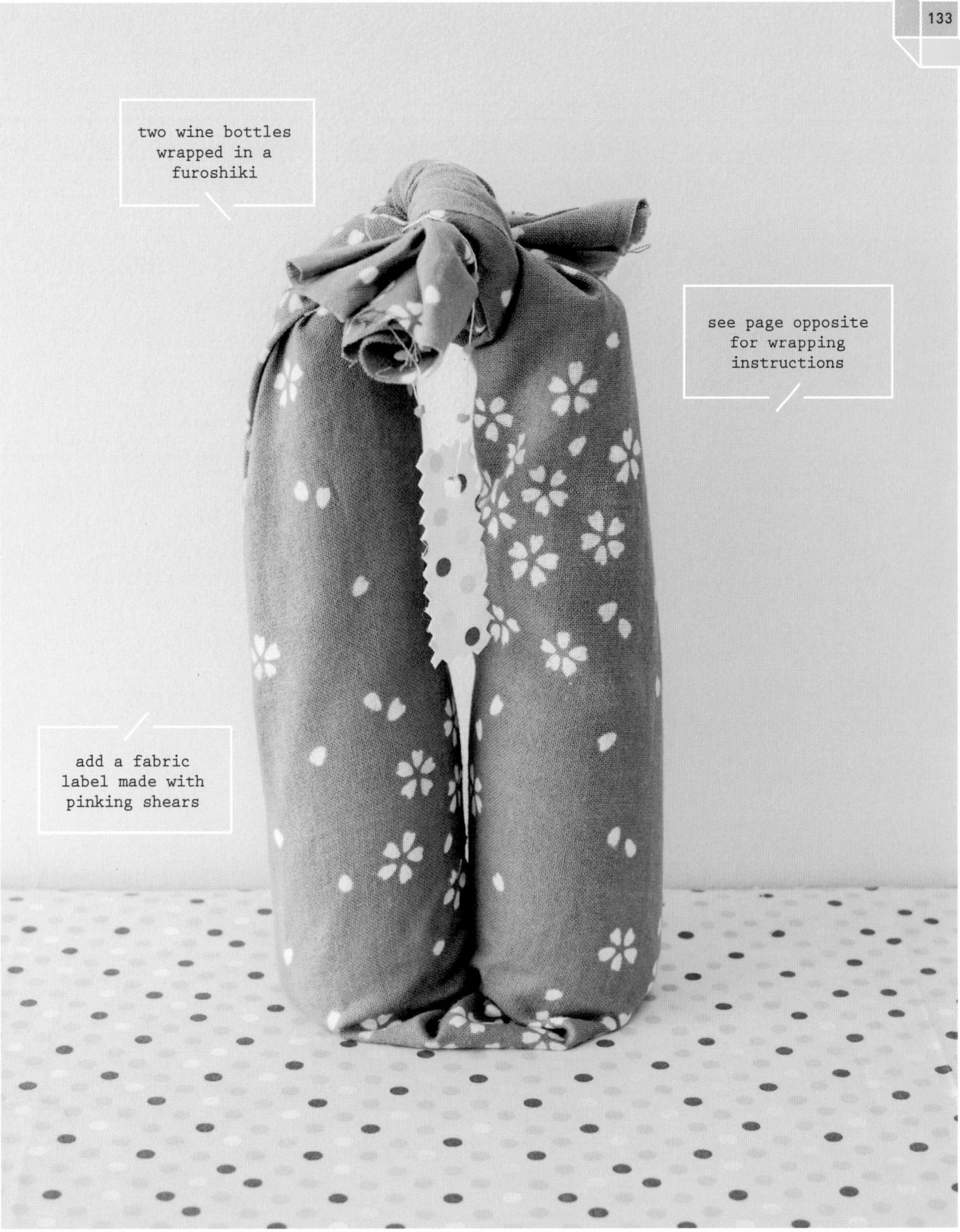

two wine bottles
wrapped in a
furoshiki

see page opposite
for wrapping
instructions

add a fabric
label made with
pinking shears

Wrapping

add some
fabric cut
with pinking
shears

this
is a perfect
way to wrap
books

Wrapping

use some
special paper
to wrap as a
bellyband
(or 'obi sash')
around your
parcel

pretty up brown
paper wrapping with
buttons and
pressed flowers

wrap items individually and then pack together

iso printed recycled papers and cloth wrapping

my friend Hiki made this parcel for me

Wrapping

EVERYDAY PAPER ITEMS

Don't stress if you haven't had time to make wrapping paper or nip out and buy it. Newspapers, flyers, magazines, vintage papers, sheet music, pages from old books, maps, train timetables, vintage sewing patterns and just about any other kind of paper item, new or used, can be utilised to wrap gifts. Try having a colour base and putting a band of unusual paper around the middle, then fastening with string.

COLOUR BLOCKING

Bold colours can make a huge impact! Try wrapping your parcel with one bright colour, then rewrap a portion of the parcel in another colour and tie it all together with a wide coloured ribbon. I think that two brights and a pastel can look lovely together, or two brights and a metallic copper, gold or bronze. Why not use black or white as a base and bring one colour in on a diagonal? Play with shapes and lines; work squares, rectangles or triangles into your design. Try matching the colour scheme to the contents of your package for a truly integrated look.

STAMP YOUR OWN PAPER OR FABRIC

Stamping paper and fabric is a fun activity that you can involve kids in, and is perfect for a crafternoon with friends. Carve your own stamps or have some made from my templates (see page 31) for some truly personalised wrapping paper or fabric wrap.

Simple designs work best, and if you have a few pretty ink colours, you can layer the design. Triangles and circles work well, as you can haphazardly place them over each other to create an interconnecting design. If you are stamping onto fabric, it's important to remember to buy fabric-specific ink and to wash your fabric before use (especially if you are wrapping food).

Before stamping your final fabric or paper, have a good play. Try some ink combinations that are a little out of the ordinary (or your comfort zone). Sometimes the imperfect or the unexpected becomes your favourite design, so don't be too precious about your placements!

a simple Japanese wrapping technique with square paper or cloth

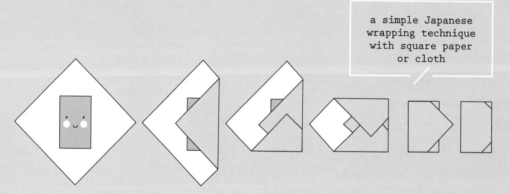

add your
loved one's
name

VELVET

many
furoshiki
cloths are
reversible

use
left-over
wrapping paper
for belly-
bands

an egg
carton
can be reused
for easter
eggs

VINTAGE PAPERS
I love to find vintage papers and advertising materials when travelling or online. It's great for wrapping special presents or using as a feature band around a brown paper package.

Wrapping

MAKE THE INSIDE COUNT
Think about how you are going
to pad your parcel, especially
if it will hold delicate items.
Shredded paper can be
functional and pretty.

Washi taping or
collaging the
interior of the
box can add an
extra layer of
wonder when the
gift is opened.

Whatever you
choose to do,
as long as any
precious items
are properly
wrapped, you can
go wild and craft
up an interior
storm.

shred bright
paper, kraft
paper and
newspaper

use washi tapes
in different
thicknesses

Tags & decorating

paper doilies
make great
additions

pleat paper
and use
fabric
buttons

choose a
colour theme
but clash the
patterns

make mutiple
components then
mix and match

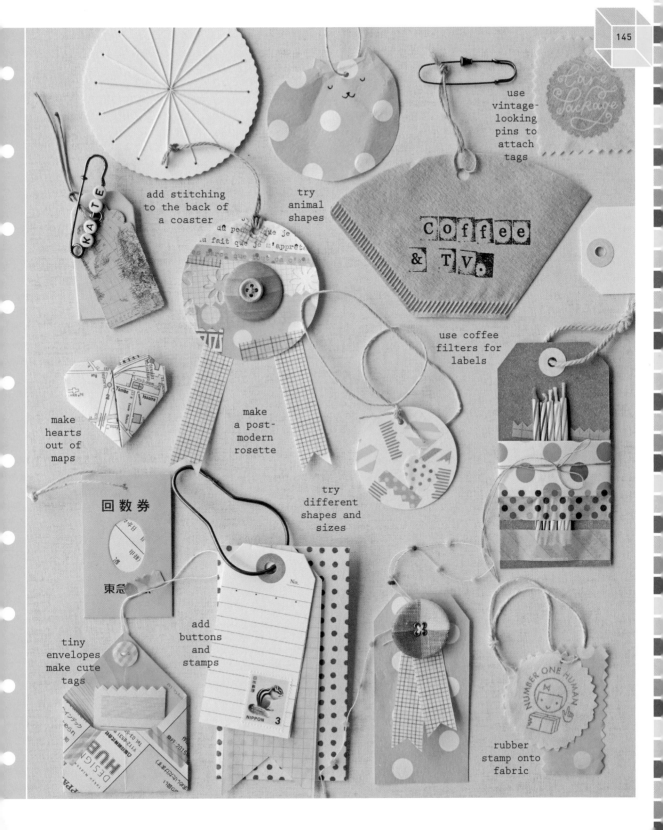

use vintage-looking pins to attach tags

Care Package

add stitching to the back of a coaster

try animal shapes

KATE

coffee & TV.

make hearts out of maps

make a post-modern rosette

use coffee filters for labels

try different shapes and sizes

回数券

東急

tiny envelopes make cute tags

add buttons and stamps

No.

NIPPON 3

DESIGN HUB

NUMBER ONE HUMAN

rubber stamp onto fabric

Templates

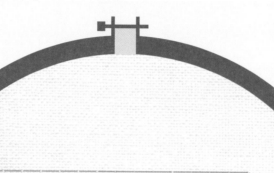
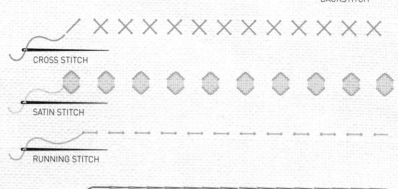

BACKSTITCH

CROSS STITCH

SATIN STITCH

RUNNING STITCH

SPLIT STITCH

BACKSTITCH

SATIN STITCH

CROSS STITCH

RUNNING STITCH

SPLIT STITCH

VISIBLE MENDING SHAPE IDEAS

HOME MADE

HOME MADE

HOME MADE

BLOW UP TO FIT ON A BAG OF YOUR CHOICE

USE AT ANY SIZE YOU LIKE!

BOX BASE

BOX WRAPAROUND

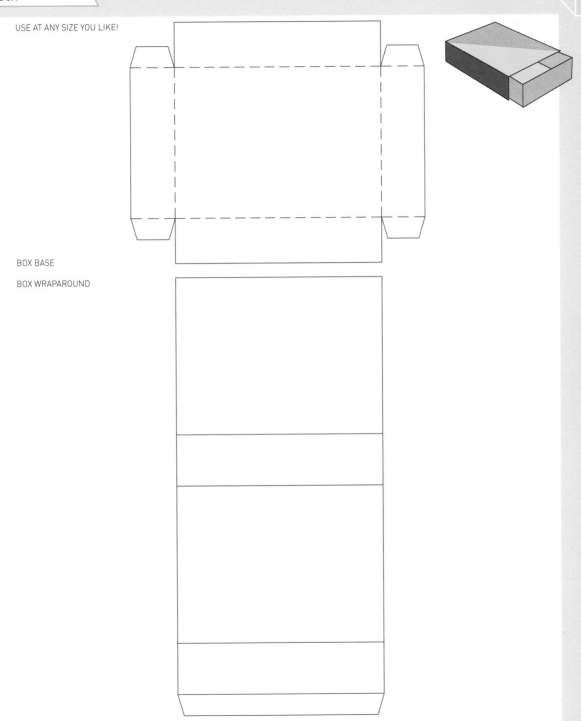

USE AT ANY SIZE YOU LIKE!

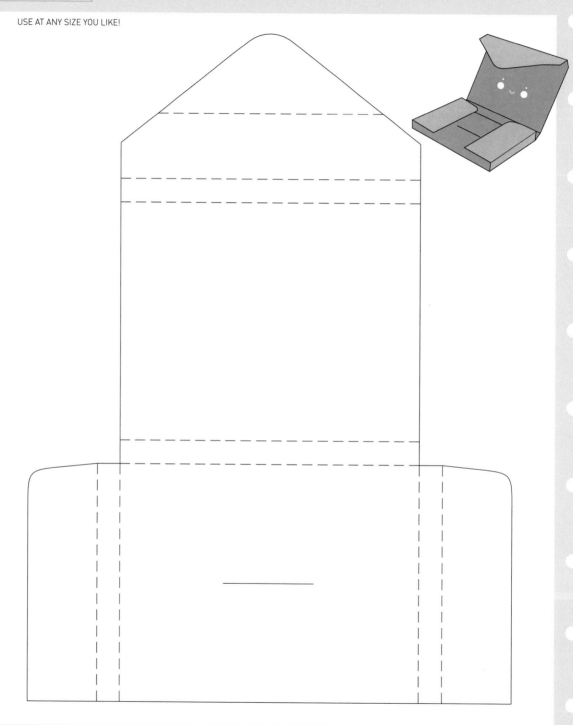

USE AT ANY SIZE YOU LIKE!

BOX LID

BOX

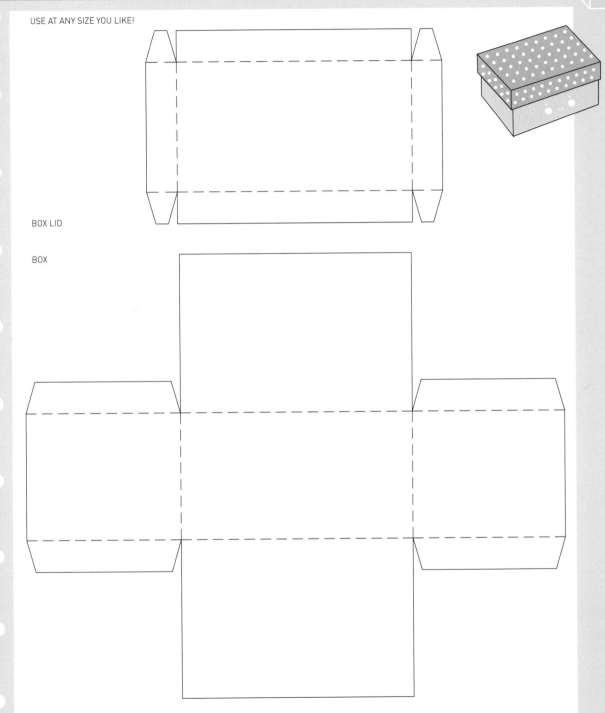

USE AT ANY SIZE YOU LIKE!

MILK CARTON

USE AT ANY SIZE YOU LIKE!

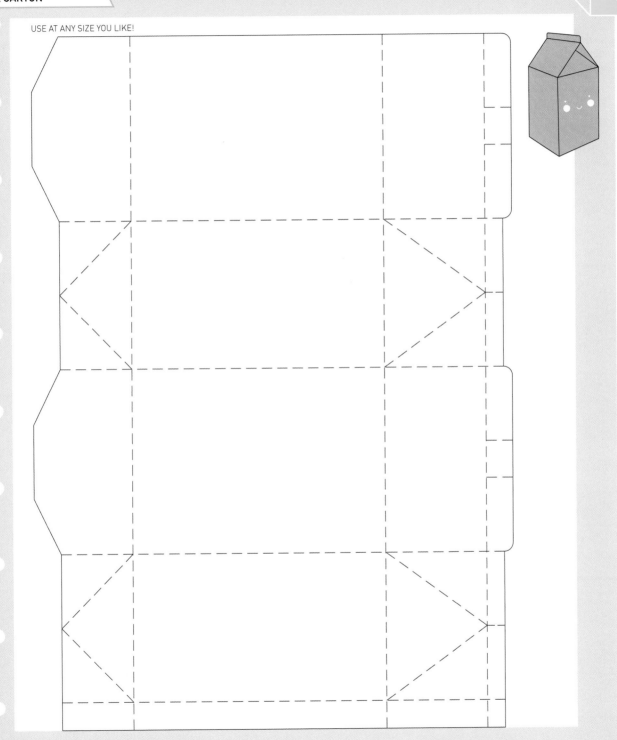

THANK YOUS
and appreciations

Thankyou to Pam Brewster for believing in this little book and helping it to find a place in this new world. Thankyou to Chris Middleton for his always exceptional photography, and to Alice Oehr for her modelling skills. Thankyou to Hisashi Tokuyoshi and Hiki Komura for their amazing Tokyo photography skills and to Coco Tashima for all her help and friendship. Thankyou to my amazing husband Steve and to my incredibly supportive family: mum, Carolyn and family, and Andrew and family.

And thankyou to all my incredibly supportive friends and to Jane Willson, Lucy Heaver and Rihana Ries who worked with me on Care Packages.

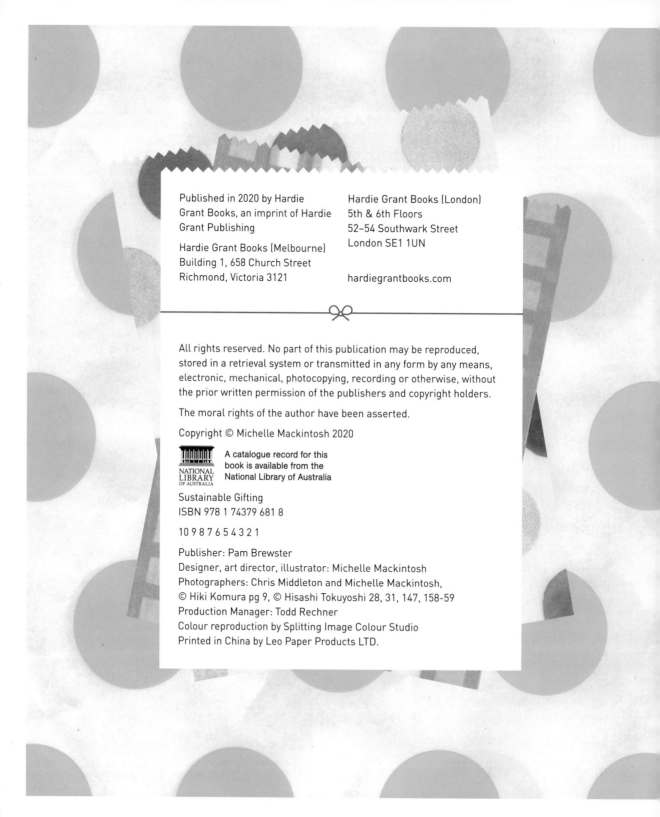

Published in 2020 by Hardie
Grant Books, an imprint of Hardie
Grant Publishing

Hardie Grant Books (Melbourne)
Building 1, 658 Church Street
Richmond, Victoria 3121

Hardie Grant Books (London)
5th & 6th Floors
52–54 Southwark Street
London SE1 1UN

hardiegrantbooks.com

A catalogue record for this
book is available from the
National Library of Australia

Sustainable Gifting
ISBN 978 1 74379 681 8

10 9 8 7 6 5 4 3 2 1

Publisher: Pam Brewster
Designer, art director, illustrator: Michelle Mackintosh
Photographers: Chris Middleton and Michelle Mackintosh,
© Hiki Komura pg 9, © Hisashi Tokuyoshi 28, 31, 147, 158-59
Production Manager: Todd Rechner
Colour reproduction by Splitting Image Colour Studio
Printed in China by Leo Paper Products LTD.

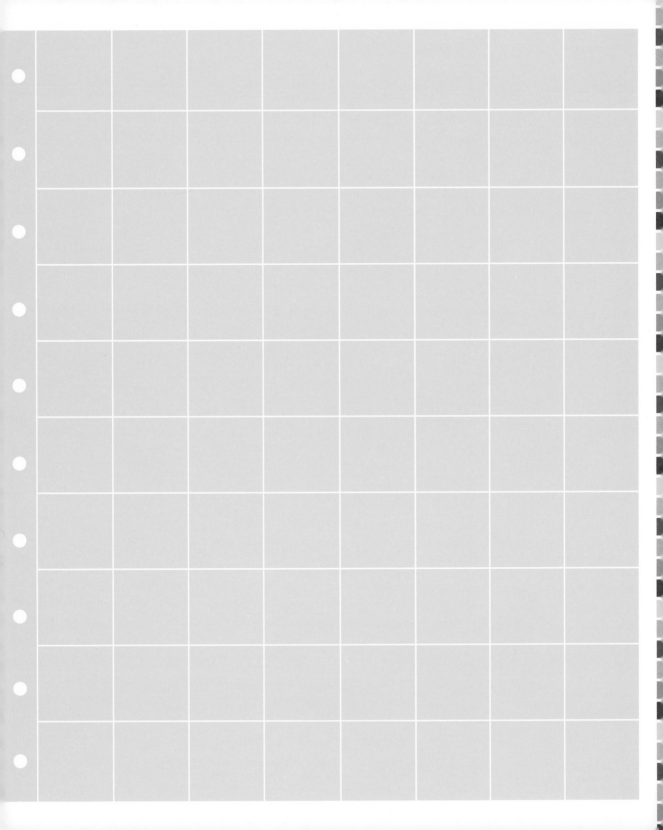